EDIBLE
PRESENTS

TO MAKE

NORMA MILLER

Contents

HELPFUL TIPS AND HINTS 3

CHAPTER ONE

Christmas and New Year 5

CHAPTER TWO

Special Days 23

CHAPTER THREE

Special Occasions 37

CHAPTER FOUR

Presents for Keeps 55

CHAPTER FIVE

Surprise Presents 63

CHAPTER SIX

Bazaars and Fêtes 79

CHAPTER SEVEN

Packaging 91

First published in 1985 by
Octopus Books Limited
as Delicious Gifts.

This edition published in 1989 by
The Hamlyn Publishing Group Limited,
a division of the Octopus Publishing Group,
Michelin House,
81 Fulham Road,
London SW3 6RB

ISBN 0 600 56470 3

Produced by Mandarin Offset.
Printed and bound in Hong Kong.

Conceived by Tricorn Publishing Ltd.

HELPFUL TIPS AND HINTS

When using liquid food colourings which are very concentrated, dip a skewer or cocktail stick into the bottle and drop small quantities on to icing or almond paste.

Allow icings and almond paste to dry completely before painting with food colourings, to prevent the colours from running. Painting dry icing with food colouring will result in a stronger colour than adding colouring at the mixing stage.

Keep a small new paintbrush in the kitchen drawer especially for using food colourings.

Keep a collection of drawings taken from old greetings cards or books. The patterns can then be used as designs for your cakes.

In spare moments use leftover egg whites to make royal icing. Colour and pipe flowers or rosettes on to waxed paper. Leave to dry for several days and store in an airtight container. These will keep for years and make an instant decoration for cakes, biscuits or sweets.

Save cardboard cereal packets to cut out shapes to use as a guide for biscuits or cakes.

STERILIZING JARS AND BOTTLES FOR STORING PRESERVES

Thoroughly wash jars and bottles with washing-up liquid, making sure that old labels are removed. Rinse and drain well. Place on their sides on the oven shelves. Close the door, set the oven to 150°C, 300°F, Gas Mark 2 and leave for 20 minutes. Wearing thick oven gloves, carefully remove the bottles and fill with a hot preserve.

NOTE: Check the jars and bottles you intend to use very carefully to make sure they are not cracked or flawed, otherwise they may shatter when a hot preserve is poured into them.

SEALING JARS AND BOTTLES

Seal preserves such as jams, cheeses, curds, marmalades and jellies by placing a waxed disc directly on top of the hot preserve. Immediately cover the warm jar with a wet cellophane circle and secure with an elastic band. The cellophane will become taut as it dries. The waxed discs, cellophane circles and elastic bands can be purchased together in one packet for jam making. Screw-topped lids can be used in place of the cellophane circles, but the waxed discs will help to prevent mould from forming.

Pickles and chutneys can be sealed with cellophane circles or plastic-coated lids. If a metal lid is used, the vinegar in the preserves will eventually eat into it.

Bottles and jars can be sealed with corks, and the tops brushed with, or dipped in, melted sealing wax.

FONDANT ICING

Makes 350g (12oz)

350g (12oz) icing sugar, sifted

1 tablespoon liquid glucose, warmed

1 egg white

1 tablespoon each icing sugar and cornflour, sifted together for kneading

Preparation time: 30 minutes
Storage time: 2 weeks, in cling film in the refrigerator

1. Place the icing sugar, warmed liquid glucose and the egg white in a mixing bowl. Cut through the ingredients with a palette knife until they are evenly mixed.
2. Turn the mixture on to a surface lightly dusted with the icing sugar and cornflour and knead the fondant until it is smooth and silky.
3. Wrap in cling film and store in the refrigerator until needed. [F]
[F] Freeze for up to 4 months. Thaw in a warm room for 3 hours still wrapped in cling film.

MARBLING FONDANT ICING OR ALMOND PASTE

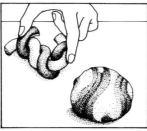

Kneading together different colours of almond paste or fondant icing to show a marbled effect.

1. Take 2 pieces of fondant icing or almond paste and, on a surface lightly dusted with cornflour, if using fondant icing, or sifted icing sugar, if using almond paste, knead a few drops of food colouring into one portion. Knead until the colour is thoroughly mixed into the icing or paste.
2. Roll the coloured and plain portions into two long sausage shapes and twist together. Roll into a ball and knead just until the colour is marbled throughout.
3. Wrap in cling film until required.

MAKING A GREASEPROOF PAPER ICING BAG

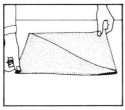

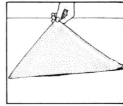

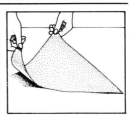

1. Cut a 20cm (8 inch) square of greaseproof paper and fold in half diagonally to form a triangle.

2. Hold the corner of paper opposite the long side between thumb and finger of the left hand.

3. Take one corner of paper in the right hand and twist up and round to meet the corner held in the left hand.

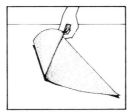

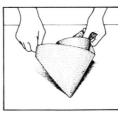

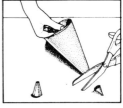

4. Form a cone shape and hold firmly in the left hand.

5. Take the remaining corner and wrap around the cone so that all the corners are together.

6. Fold over or staple the points. Snip off the end and drop in an icing nozzle.

CHAPTER ONE

Christmas and New Year

During the festive season we brighten each other's lives by giving more presents than at any other time. As a change, put your culinary skills to use, producing delicious edible gifts from the following selection.

Mini Christmas Cakes

Makes six 10 cm (4 inch) cakes

Cake:

100 g (4 oz) plain flour
100 g (4 oz) self-raising flour
1 teaspoon mixed spice
1/2 teaspoon ground nutmeg
1/4 teaspoon ground cinnamon
175 g (6 oz) dark brown sugar
175 g (6 oz) butter, softened
100 g (4 oz) sultanas
mixed dried fruit
100 g (4 oz) cherries, washed, dried and quartered
100 g (4 oz) walnuts, roughly chopped
100 g (4 oz) ground almonds
1/2 teaspoon almond essence
4 tablespoons milk or sherry
grated rind of 1 lemon
3 eggs

To decorate:

2 tablespoons apricot jam, warmed and sieved
275 g (10 oz) almond paste
4 egg whites
1 kg (2 lb) icing sugar, sifted, plus extra, for dusting
red, green, yellow and orange food colourings

Preparation time: 2 hours, plus 2 1/2 days' drying
Cooking time: 1 1/2 hours
Oven: 150°C, 300°F, Gas Mark 2
Storage time: 4 weeks, in an airtight container

Make these cakes 3 months in advance to allow the flavour to mature and pour over a little sherry each month.

1. Grease and line six 10 cm (4 inch) round cake tins.
2. Sift the flours, mixed spice, nutmeg and cinnamon into a large bowl. Add the remaining cake ingredients and beat together with a wooden spoon until thoroughly combined, about 5 minutes.
3. Divide the mixture between the prepared tins. Smooth the tops with the back of a wet metal spoon and make a slight hollow in the middle.
4. Cook in a preheated oven for 1 1/2 hours until golden and a warm skewer pushed in the middle of the cake comes out clean. Leave in the tins for 15 minutes before turning out on to a wire tray. Remove the lining paper, and cool.
5. To decorate, brush the tops of the cakes with the warm, sieved apricot jam.
6. Roll out the almond paste on a surface lightly dusted with icing sugar to a thickness of about 5 mm (1/4 inch). Cut out six 10 cm (4 inch) circles and reserve the trimmings. Place the almond paste circles on top of the cakes and leave to dry for 1 day.
7. Place the egg whites in a bowl and beat with a fork to break them up a little. Add the 1 kg (2 lb) icing sugar, a little at a time, beating well with a wooden spoon between each addition. Continue beating until the icing has whitened and become stiff. Cover with a damp cloth until needed.
8. Secure the cakes to silver cake boards with a little of the icing. Using a palette knife, spread a little icing on top of each cake and smooth over to remove any air bubbles. Draw a clean metal ruler across the icing to leave a flat surface and remove any surplus icing with a sharp knife. Leave to dry for 12 hours in a warm place, then coat with another layer of icing.
9. Look at Christmas cards for ideas to decorate the cakes using the remaining almond paste and royal icing and decorate with food colourings (see the photograph on right). Allow the icing to dry for 24 hours.
10. Tie a ribbon or cake frill around each cake and pack into tins or boxes, or overwrap in cellophane paper. Tie with ribbon and label.

Edible Christmas Card

Makes 1 card

175 g (6 oz) fondant icing (page 4)

1 tablespoon grated orange rind

1 teaspoon coffee essence

1 tablespoon desiccated coconut

2 tablespoons cornflour

blue, green, red, yellow and orange food colourings

75 g (3 oz) icing sugar, sifted

Preparation time: 1 hour, plus drying
Storage time: 2 months, in an airtight container

1. Knead 100 g (4 oz) of the fondant icing, the orange rind, coffee essence and coconut together.
2. On a surface dusted with cornflour, roll the icing to a 15 cm (6 inch) square. Lift with a palette knife on to a board.
3. Cut the remaining fondant in half. Roll out 1 portion and cut out a triangle and a small oblong to form a Christmas tree. Moisten one side of the shapes with water and press on to the fondant base.
4. Shape the rest of the fondant into small squares and oblongs to represent parcels. Moisten with water and arrange along the bottom of the card.
5. With food colourings paint the card, the tree, and some of the parcels. Leave to dry for 3 hours.
6. Place the icing sugar in a bowl, add water a few drops at a time and beat with a wooden spoon until thick and smooth.
7. Use a tablespoon of icing (see page 4) to pipe a greeting on the tree. Colour a teaspoon of icing yellow and pipe dots on the tree. Colour the remaining icing red and use to pipe dots and loops on the tree, a border around the card and crosses to represent string on the larger parcels. Leave to dry for 6 hours, then pack in a box.

Cake Plaques

Makes 4

225 g (8 oz) fondant icing
(page 4)

100 g (4 oz) almond paste

food colourings of your choice

100 g (4 oz) icing sugar, sifted,
plus extra, for dusting

Preparation time: 1 hour, plus 1 week's drying
Storage time: 6 months, in an airtight container

These plaques are ideal for the busy cook to use as an instant decoration on top of birthday or celebration cakes.
You can decorate the plaques with almond paste shapes, as described in the recipe, or if you prefer, you can pipe a name or message across the top. Either way, the plaques will transform a plain cake into a special creation.

1. Divide the fondant icing into 4 portions and colour each piece with a few drops of different coloured food colourings.
2. On a surface dusted with icing sugar roll each portion of fondant to a thickness of not less than 5 mm (¼ inch) and shape the 4 pieces into rounds, squares, ovals, oblongs, or one of each shape. Flute the edges with the prongs of a fork, metal crimpers or pinch between finger and thumb (see illustrations on page 11).
3. Using a fish slice, carefully lift each shape on to a tray covered with non-stick silicone paper, cover with a cloth and leave to dry in a warm place for 6 days.
4. Knead a few drops of food colouring into the almond paste. Turn on to a surface dusted with icing sugar and roll out. Using tiny pastry cutters, cut into shapes such as stars, leaves, flowers, triangles.
5. Place the icing sugar in a bowl, add a little water a few drops at a time and beat with a wooden spoon until thick and smooth. Attach the almond paste shapes to the fondant plaques with a little of the icing. Leave to dry for 1 day.
6. Pack the plaques into a box with a strip of cardboard between each. Tie with ribbon and label.

(Pictured on page 10.)

Edible Christmas card

Christmas Gift Tags

Makes 8

450 g (1 lb) icing sugar, sifted, plus extra, for dusting

1 egg white, lightly beaten

1 ½ tablespoons double or whipping cream

2 teaspoons peppermint essence

blue, red, green, orange or yellow food colourings

ribbon

Preparation time: 40 minutes, plus 8 days' drying
Storage time: 1 month, in an airtight container

Pens containing food colourings are now available from cookshops. These can be used to write messages on the tags.

1. Place the icing sugar in a large bowl and add half the beaten egg white, the cream and peppermint essence. Beat with a wooden spoon until very stiff and smooth, adding more egg white if necessary.
2. On a surface dusted with icing sugar, knead the mixture until smooth.
3. Roll to form a 20 cm (8 inch) square which is not less than 5 mm (¼ inch) thick, then cut into oblongs measuring 5 × 10 cm (2 × 4 inches).
4. Lift the oblongs carefully with a fish slice on to a tray covered with non-stick silicone paper. Push a small hole in one corner with the end of a piping tube.
5. Either leave the labels plain, or flute the edges by pinching between thumb and finger, or press with the prongs of a fork, or pinch with fondant crimpers. Cover with a cloth and leave to dry in a warm place for 1 week.
6. Using a clean paintbrush and the food colourings paint patterns around the edges or lines across the labels. Leave to dry for 1 day, and then add a message in food colouring. When dry thread a length of brightly coloured ribbon through the holes and attach to presents, or pack into boxes between layers of tissue paper.

Cake plaques (recipe on page 9); Christmas gift tag

Cutting a hole with the end of a piping tube

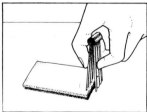

Crimping the edges with fondant crimpers

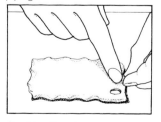

Pinching the edges

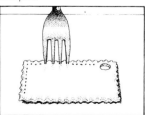

Decorating with a fork

Mini Plum Puddings

Makes 6

75 g (3 oz) wholewheat flour
75 g (3 oz) self-raising flour
½ teaspoon salt
½ teaspoon ground ginger
¼ teaspoon ground mace
¼ teaspoon ground nutmeg
175 g (6 oz) brown breadcrumbs
75 g (3 oz) suet
75 g (3 oz) grated carrot
100 g (4 oz) dark brown sugar
275 g (10 oz) raisins
175 g (6 oz) currants
75 g (3 oz) sultanas
50 g (2 oz) dates, chopped
50 g (2 oz) dried figs, chopped
25 g (1 oz) candied peel
75 g (3 oz) mixed nuts, roughly chopped
100 g (4 oz) grated cooking apple
grated rind of 1 lemon
4 tablespoons lemon juice
2 eggs
2 tablespoons white or dark rum
150 ml (¼ pint) milk

Preparation time: 1 hour, plus standing overnight
Cooking time: 3 hours, plus 1½ hours before eating
Storage time: 6 months

These puddings can be made up to 3 months in advance and stored in a cool place: the flavour improves with standing. Steam in batches if you have a large enough pan, or in a pressure cooker, which will reduce the cooking time. If you prefer darker puddings, steam for longer than the specified time.

You might like to give a miniature bottle of rum with each pudding; the rum can either be used to make a sauce or can be poured over the pudding and ignited. Alternatively, you could give a jar of Orange Brandy Butter (see right) as an accompanying gift.

1. Sift together the flours, salt and spices in a mixing bowl. Add all the other ingredients, except the milk, and mix until thoroughly combined.
2. Add enough milk to give a dropping consistency. If the mixture is dry, add a little more. Cover the bowl with a clean cloth and leave to stand overnight.
3. Pack the mixture into 6 greased 300 ml (½ pint) basins. Cover with greased greaseproof paper and foil and secure with string.
4. Steam over boiling water for 3 hours, topping up the water as necessary. Allow to cool and replace the greaseproof paper, foil and string.
5. Wrap in cling film or cellophane and tie with ribbon. Label with the cooking instructions, and add a sprig of holly.
6. To serve, steam the puddings over boiling water for a further 1½ hours. Hand Brandy butter (see right) or white rum sauce separately.

Mini plum puddings; Orange brandy butter

Orange Brandy Butter

Makes 1 kg (2 lb)

225 g (8 oz) unsalted butter

750 g (1 ½ lb) icing sugar, sifted

grated rind of 1 orange

2 tablespoons orange juice

2 tablespoons brandy

Preparation time: 30 minutes
Storage time: 6 weeks, in a refrigerator

1. Beat the butter in a mixing bowl until light and fluffy. Gradually add the icing sugar, mixing until smooth.
2. Stir in the orange rind, juice and brandy.
3. Spoon or pipe into small jars. Cover with cling film or a jam pot cover. Tie ribbon around the neck of the jar and attach a label.

Tunis Cake

Makes one 18 cm (7 inch) cake

Cake:

225 g (8 oz) plain flour

1½ teaspoons baking powder

175 g (6 oz) butter, softened

175 g (6 oz) caster sugar

3 eggs

1 teaspoon almond essence

To decorate:

100 g (4 oz) plain chocolate, broken into pieces

50 g (2 oz) almond paste

yellow, orange, green and red food colourings

1 tablespoon sugar

Preparation time: 1 hour
Cooking time: 1½-1¾ hours
Oven: 160°C, 325°F, Gas Mark 3
Storage time: 2 weeks, in an airtight container

1. Grease and line an 18 cm (7 inch) round cake tin.
2. Sift the flour with the baking powder, place all the cake ingredients in a mixing bowl and beat with a wooden spoon until the mixture is light and fluffy. Pour into the prepared cake tin.
3. Bake in a preheated oven for 1½-1¾ hours. Leave in the tin for 2-3 minutes before turning out. ꄷF
4. To decorate, place on a cake board and wrap a band of greaseproof paper around the cake which stands 2½ cm (1 inch) above the top of the cake.
5. Place the chocolate in a bowl over a pan of hot water and heat gently until the chocolate has melted. Reserve 1 teaspoon of the melted chocolate and spread the remainder on top of the cake and allow to cool.
6. When the chocolate is completely set, carefully peel the greaseproof paper away from the sides of the cake.
7. Model the almond paste into a selection of mini fruits: apples, oranges, bananas, grapes, pears. Paint with the food colouring and roll in the sugar.
8. Arrange the fruits on top of the cake, using the remaining melted chocolate to attach them. Place a cake frill around the cake.
9. Pack into a box, tie with ribbon and attach a label.
F Freeze for up to 4 months. Thaw for 4 hours at room temperature and decorate.

Scottish Black Bun

Preparation time: 50 minutes, plus chilling
Cooking time: 1 hour 40 minutes
Oven: 200°C, 400°F, Gas Mark 6
then: 160°C, 325°F, Gas Mark 3
Storage time: 3 weeks, in an airtight container

Makes one 1 kg (2 lb) loaf

Pastry:

350 g (12 oz) plain flour, sifted

175 g (6 oz) white fat, softened

water

Filling:

100 g (4 oz) plain flour

4 teaspoons mixed spice

175 g (6 oz) dark brown sugar

175 g (6 oz) currants

175 g (6 oz) sultanas

100 g (4 oz) mixed peel

100 g (4 oz) almonds, chopped

50 g (2 oz) margarine, softened

grated rind of 2 lemons

4 eggs, beaten

4 teaspoons black treacle

4 teaspoons whisky

---

1. Place the flour in a mixing bowl and rub in the white fat until the mixture resembles fine breadcrumbs. Add just enough water to form a firm dough.
2. Knead lightly on a floured surface and chill, covered with cling film, for 30 minutes.
3. Roll three-quarters of the pastry on a floured surface and use to line a non-stick 1 kg (2 lb) loaf tin.
4. To make the filling, sift the flour with the mixed spice, then mix all the filling ingredients together in a bowl and beat for 2 minutes until thoroughly combined. Pack the filling into the loaf tin and press down well.
5. Roll the remaining pastry to fit the top of the loaf tin. Brush the edges of the pastry with water and place the pastry lid in position. Pinch and trim the edges.
6. Roll out the trimmings and cut out leaf or thistle shapes. Brush the top of the bun with a little water and attach the decorations.
7. Bake in a preheated oven for 15 minutes. Lower the oven temperature and bake for a further 1 hour 25 minutes.
8. Leave to cool in the tin. Wrap the tin in cellophane and decorate with ribbon.

Tropical Relish

Makes approximately 3½ kg (8 lb)

1 mango, skinned and chopped
1 pawpaw, skinned and chopped
750 g (1½ lb) cooking apples, skinned, cored and chopped
450 g (1 lb) onions, peeled and chopped
450 g (1 lb) damsons or plums, stoned and chopped
225 g (8 oz) sultanas
100 g (4 oz) raisins
100 g (4 oz) dates, chopped
900 ml (1½ pints) distilled white vinegar
450 g (1 lb) sugar
40 g (1½ oz) salt
10 g (¼ oz) fresh ginger, peeled and grated
10 g (¼ oz) whole allspice, tied in a piece of muslin
10 g (¼ oz) ground black pepper

Preparation time: 40 minutes
Cooking time: 1 hour 20 minutes
Storage: 1 year

This relish is delicious served with barbecued food such as steaks, kebabs or chicken drumsticks. It can also be used to liven up a basic stuffing mix, or as an accompaniment to baked fish or savoury pancakes.

1. Place all the ingredients in a preserving pan or a large heavy-based pan. Heat slowly until the sugar has dissolved.
2. Bring to the boil and simmer for 1 hour 20 minutes, stirring occasionally, until the mixture is very thick. Remove the muslin bag of spices.
3. Pour into hot sterilized pots or jars (see page 3) and cover with plastic-coated lids.
4. Label and cover the lids with circles of fabric tied with ribbon.

Hot Indian Pickle

Makes approximately 750 g (1½ lb)

2 tablespoons coriander seeds
1 tablespoon black mustard seeds
15 g (½ oz) salt
1 tablespoon asafoetida (optional) (see below)
600 ml (1 pint) distilled white vinegar

Preparation time: 30 minutes
Cooking time: 1 hour
Storage time: 1 year

Asafoetida will give a distinctive taste to this pickle; it is available from health shops, delicatessens and shops selling Indian food. The same quantity of curry powder can be used as an alternative, but the same flavour will not be achieved.

1. Tie the coriander seeds and half of the mustard seeds in a piece of muslin. Place in a preserving pan or a heavy-based pan with the remaining mustard seeds, salt, asafoetida (if using), 300 ml (½ pint) of the vinegar and 100 g (4 oz) of the sugar, the mangoes and chillies.
2. Heat slowly until the sugar has dissolved. Bring to the boil and simmer.

225 g (8 oz) sugar

1 kg (2 lb) mangoes, peeled and thinly sliced

4 red chillies, seeded and finely chopped

1 tablespoon cornflour

stirring occasionally with a wooden spoon, until the mangoes have softened, about 40 minutes. Remove the muslin bag of spices.

3. Drain the mangoes and measure the juices. There should be about 300 ml (½ pint); if there is less, make up to this quantity with water.

4. Return the juices to the pan with the remaining vinegar and sugar. Bring to the boil, stirring constantly, and cook until the syrup has reduced to 300 ml (½ pint).

5. Blend the cornflour to a smooth paste with a little of the syrup. Add the blended cornflour and mango mixture to the syrup. Bring to the boil and cook, stirring, for 2 minutes.

6. Pour into sterilized pots or jars (see page 3) and cover with plastic-coated lids.

7. Label and cover the lids with circles of fabric tied with ribbon.

Left: Tropical relish; **Right:** Hot Indian pickle

Blackberry vinegar; Sloe gin; Candied pumpkin

Blackberry Vinegar

Preparation time: 30 minutes, plus 4 days' standing
Cooking time: 40 minutes
Storage time: 1 year

Makes 2.25 litres (4 pints)

1 kg (2 lb) blackberries, washed and dried

1.2 litres (2 pints) distilled vinegar

sugar (see right)

---

1. Place the blackberries and vinegar in a large glass bowl, cover and leave for 4 days. Stir with a wooden spoon every day.
2. Measure the juice and pour into a pan with 450 g (1 lb) sugar for every 600 ml (1 pint) juice.
3. Heat very slowly, stirring all the time, until the sugar has dissolved. Bring to the boil and simmer for 15 minutes.
4. Strain the vinegar into sterilized bottles (see page 3), seal with corks or plastic-coated lids and label. Store in a cool place.

Sloe or Raspberry Gin

Makes approximately 1.2 litres (2 pints)

450 g (1 lb) sloes, stalks removed, or 450 g (1 lb) raspberries

175 g (6 oz) sugar

100 g (4 oz) flaked almonds

900 ml (1 ½ pints) gin

Preparation time: 40 minutes, plus 6 months' standing and maturing
Storage time: 1 year

1. If using sloes, pierce the skins with a darning needle or skewer.
2. Layer the sloes or raspberries, sugar and almonds in a large glass jar, or bottle Pour over the gin.
3. Seal tightly and leave for 3 days in a light warm room, shaking the jar every day. Transfer to a dark place for 3 months.
4. Strain the liquor, pour into sterilized bottles (see page 3), seal and label. Leave to mature for 3 months before use.
5. The discarded fruit can be simmered with a little sugar and served with cream as a dessert.

Candied Pumpkin

Makes approximately 450 g (1 lb)

450 g (1 lb) sugar, plus 3 tablespoons

65 ml (2 ½ fl oz) water

450 g (1 lb) pumpkin, peeled and cubed

coloured sugar crystals (optional)

Preparation time: 30 minutes, plus marinating and drying overnight
Cooking time: 10-15 minutes
Storage time: 2 weeks

1. Place the 450 g (1 lb) sugar and the water in a pan and heat gently, stirring with a metal spoon, until the sugar has dissolved. (The spoon will get very hot, so be sure to wear an oven glove.) Add the cubed pumpkin and cook for 10-15 minutes until just tender.
2. Remove the pumpkin with a slotted spoon and reserve. Boil the remaining liquid until it has reduced by half. Pour the syrup into a bowl, add the pumpkin, cover and leave for 6 hours.
3. Place a wire tray over a baking sheet or tray. Drain the pumpkin, reserving the syrup and place on the wire tray. Coat the pumpkin with the remaining syrup every hour until used up. Leave the pumpkin to dry in a warm place for 24 hours.
4. Toss the pumpkin cubes in the 3 tablespoons of sugar or, for an extra sparkle, use the coloured sugar crystals.
5. Pack into small tins or boxes, then tie with ribbon and label.

Whisky Mincemeat

Makes approximately 2¾ kg (6 lb)

225 g (8 oz) suet
450 g (1 lb) muscovado sugar
450 g (1 lb) firm apples, peeled, cored and grated
450 g (1 lb) raisins
350 g (12 oz) currants
350 g (12 oz) sultanas
225 g (8 oz) glacé cherries, quartered
100 g (4 oz) glacé pineapple, chopped
100 g (4 oz) angelica, chopped
100 g (4 oz) mixed peel
100 g (4 oz) mixed nuts, roughly chopped
grated rind of 2 lemons
6 tablespoons lemon juice
150 ml (¼ pint) whisky

Preparation time: 30 minutes, plus 2 weeks' maturing
Storage time: 6 months

You can either give this delicious mincemeat in prettily decorated jars or use it in home-made mince pies and give these as tasty presents.

Alternatively, make a large mince pie, dust with icing sugar and cut into triangles for an attractive presentation.

The mincemeat can also be used as a filling for sweet pancakes, a stuffing for baked apples or a topping for steamed puddings.

1. Place all the prepared ingredients in a large bowl and mix until thoroughly combined.
2. Cover with cling film and leave for 2 weeks to 'mature', stirring occasionally.
3. Pack into sterilized jars (see page 3), cover, seal and label. Tie coloured ribbon or string around the jars.

Spiced Oranges

Makes three 1¼ kg (3 lb) jars

1¼ kg (3 lb) oranges, satsumas or clementines
1 kg (2 lb) sugar
300 ml (½ pint) white wine vinegar
150 ml (¼ pint) water
10 cloves
2 × 7½ cm (3 inch) cinnamon sticks

Preparation time: 1 hour
Cooking time: approximately 1 hour
Storage time: 1 year

1. Thinly slice the oranges, or, if using satsumas or clementines, leave them whole.
2. Place in a large pan, cover with water, bring to the boil and simmer until the oranges are tender, about 10-15 minutes. Drain thoroughly.
3. In a large pan put the sugar, vinegar, water, cloves and cinnamon sticks. Heat gently, stirring until the sugar has dissolved. Bring to the boil and cook until the liquid has reduced by half.
4. Add the drained orange slices or whole oranges and boil for 10 minutes.
5. Pack the mixture into hot sterilized jars (see page 3). Cover with plastic-coated lids, label and decorate.
6. Serve with cold meats or pâté.

Peaches in Brandy

Makes approximately three 450 g (1 lb) jars

1 ¼ kg (3 lb) peaches
1 kg (2 ¼ lb) caster sugar
900 ml (1 ½ pints) water
450 ml (¾ pint) brandy

Spiced oranges; Peaches in brandy; Whisky mincemeat

Preparation time: 40 minutes
Cooking time: 40 minutes
Storage time: 1 year, if unopened

1. Drop the peaches into boiling water for 5 seconds, then drain. Carefully peel the skin with a sharp knife. Cut the peaches in half and remove the stones.
2. Put the sugar and water in a large pan. Heat slowly, stirring with a metal spoon, until the sugar has dissolved. Bring to the boil and continue boiling for 10 minutes.
3. Reduce the heat, add the peach halves and simmer for 5 minutes. Remove the fruit from the syrup and pack into hot sterilized jars (see page 3).
4. Boil the syrup for 5 minutes, then add the brandy. Pour carefully over the peaches in the jars.
5. Cover and seal the jars. Label and decorate with ribbon.

Orange Turkish Delight

Makes 36 pieces

300 ml (½ pint) water

grated rind of 2 oranges

grated rind of 1 lemon

40 g (1½ oz) gelatine

450 g (1 lb) sugar

4 tablespoons orange juice

2 tablespoons orange flower water

225 g (8 oz) icing sugar, sifted

2 tablespoons cornflour

Preparation time: 20 minutes, plus setting overnight
Cooking time: 20 minutes
Storage time: 2 weeks

1. Place 150 ml (¼ pint) of the water and the orange and lemon rind in a pan. Bring to the boil and simmer for 10 minutes.
2. In a separate pan, boil the remaining water and pour into a small basin. Sprinkle over the gelatine and stir until dissolved.
3. Lower the heat under the pan and add the sugar, dissolved gelatine, orange juice and orange flower water. Stir with a metal spoon until the sugar has dissolved. Bring to the boil and continue boiling for 10 minutes.
4. Strain into a wetted 18 cm (7 inch) square tin. Allow to cool and leave overnight to set.
5. Mix together the icing sugar and cornflour and sprinkle a thin layer on to a work surface.
6. With a wet knife loosen the edges of the Turkish delight. Dip the base of the tin into hot water for 4 seconds and turn the delight out on to the icing sugar and cornflour mixture.
7. Cut into 36 pieces, place in a polythene bag with the remaining sugar mixture and shake to coat the pieces thoroughly.
8. Pack into wooden boxes, or tins, between sheets of non-stick silicone paper, sprinkling any sugar mixture left in the polythene bag over each layer.
9. Tie the boxes with ribbon and label.

CHAPTER TWO

Special Days

Here you will find delicious recipes for gifts for Valentine's Day, Mother's and Father's Days, Easter and Halloween to surprise and delight your family and friends throughout the year.

Oaty Hearts

Makes approximately 8

100 g (4 oz) self-raising flour

½ teaspoon ground ginger

75 g (3 oz) butter

100 g (4 oz) fined rolled oats

75 g (3 oz) caster sugar

1 egg, beaten

2 teaspoons milk

To decorate:

2 tablespoons apricot jam

100 g (4 oz) fondant icing
(page 4)

pink or orange food colouring

Preparation time: 40 minutes
Cooking time: 15-20 minutes
Oven: 180°C, 350°F, Gas Mark 4
Storage time: 2 weeks, in an airtight container

1. Sift the flour and ground ginger into a bowl. Rub in the butter until the mixture resembles fine breadcrumbs.
2. Stir in the rolled oats and caster sugar. Add the beaten egg and milk and mix to a stiff dough.
3. Turn on to a lightly floured surface and knead until smooth.
4. Roll out to a thickness of 5 mm (¼ inch), cut into different-sized heart shapes using metal cutters or a cardboard shape. With a skewer make a hole near the top of each biscuit.
5. Place on a greased baking sheet and bake for 15-20 minutes near the top of a preheated oven until golden brown. Cool on a wire tray.
6. To decorate, knead a few drops of food colouring into half the fondant icing. Leave the other half plain. Knead the 2 portions of fondant icing together until the colour is swirled rather than mixed.
7. Turn on to a work surface dusted with sifted icing sugar and roll out thinly. Cut into heart shapes slightly smaller than the biscuits.
8. Brush each biscuit with apricot jam and cover with a fondant heart. Leave to dry for at least 3 hours.
9. Thread ribbon through the hole in each biscuit and tie a bow, or link all the biscuits together in a chain.
10. Pack into airtight containers. Label.

Liqueur Cherry Surprises

Makes 18

9 glacé cherries, halved
50 g (2 oz) raisins, chopped
3 tablespoons Cointreau
100 g (4 oz) plain chocolate, broken into pieces
100 g (4 oz) milk chocolate, broken into pieces
75 g (3 oz) almonds, toasted and chopped
1 teaspoon grated orange rind
fondant boxes (page 94)

Preparation time: 2 hours, plus 12 hours' standing
Cooking time: 10 minutes
Storage time: 10 days, in an airtight container

If you wish, use a heart-shaped mould (pictured on page 93) to make a fondant box.

1. Place the glacé cherries, raisins and Cointreau in a screw-top jar. Leave for 12 hours, shaking the jar occasionally.
2. Melt the plain chocolate in a bowl over a pan of hot water. Using the back of a teaspoon or a clean pastry brush, coat the insides of 18 petit four cases with a layer of melted chocolate. Allow to set in the refrigerator, then coat with another layer of chocolate. Chill until set firm.
3. Carefully peel the paper cases away from the chocolate shapes and replace with fresh paper cases. Place half a marinated cherry in the base of each chocolate cup.
4. Melt the milk chocolate as for the plain. Stir in the almonds, soaked raisins and orange rind. Divide the nutty mixture between the chocolate cases and leave to set in the refrigerator.
5. Pack into the fondant boxes to make a really edible present. Decorate with ribbons and attach a label.

Lip-shaped Biscuits

Makes approximately 12

50 g (2 oz) caster sugar
50 g (2 oz) butter, softened
1 egg yolk
100 g (4 oz) plain flour, sifted with a pinch of salt

Glacé icing:

1 - 1 ½ tablespoons warm water
100 g (4 oz) icing sugar, sifted
red food colouring
2 tablespoons coloured sugar crystals

Preparation time: 1 hour
Cooking time: 10-12 minutes
Oven: 200°C, 400°F, Gas Mark 6
Storage time: 3 weeks, in an airtight container

1. To make a cardboad template to use as a cutting guide for the biscuits, cut an oblong of cardboard 5 × 10 cm (2 × 4 inches). Draw a pair of lips to fill the cardboard and cut out the shape.
2. Cream together the sugar and butter in a mixing bowl until light and fluffy, then beat in the egg yolk.
3. Work in the flour and knead until smooth. Turn on to a lightly floured surface and roll out to a 5 mm (¼ inch) thickness.
4. Using the cardboard template as a guide, cut out lip shapes and place on a greased baking sheet. Re-roll the trimmings to make more biscuits.
5. Bake in a preheated oven for 10-12 minutes. Allow to cool. F
6. To make the glacé icing, beat sufficient warm water into the icing sugar to make a thick, smooth icing. Add enough food colouring to turn the mixture a deep red.
7. Spread the icing over the biscuits and sprinkle over the sugar crystals. Leave to set for 2 hours.
8. Pack into boxes and tie with ribbon.
F Freeze for up to 3 months. Thaw for 3 hours at room temperature, and decorate.

Cutting out the lip shapes and icing the biscuits

Sweets in a Shell

Makes 1 container, plus sweets

1 scallop shell, thoroughly cleaned

½ teaspoon oil

100 g (4 oz) fondant icing (page 4)

cornflour, for rolling

Sweets:

50 (2 oz) plain chocolate, broken into pieces

25 g (1 oz) sugared almonds

4 brazil nuts

6 strawberries

15 g (½ oz) pistachio nuts, finely chopped

Preparation time: 1 hour, plus at least 1 week's drying
Storage time: Fondant shell: 1 year
Almonds and nuts: 2 weeks
Strawberries: eat on the same day

1. Brush the inside of the shell with oil.
2. Knead the fondant icing on a surface dusted with cornflour and roll to a round large enough to cover the shell. Lift the fondant icing on to the shell and press into the hollow, trimming any excess with a knife. Using a cocktail stick, make lines in the icing from the centre to the edge.
3. Pinch the edge of the fondant between thumb and finger to neaten the edge. Cover with a cloth and leave to dry in a warm place for 1 week, then check to see if the icing is completely dry. Leave for a few more days if necessary.
4. To make the sweets, put the chocolate in a small basin over a pan of hot water and heat gently until melted.
5. Cover a tray with a sheet of non-stick silicone paper. Dip the almonds, nuts and strawberries in the chocolate until half covered, shaking off any excess chocolate. Place on the paper and sprinkle with the chopped pistachio nuts. Leave to dry for 3 hours.
6. Warm the scallop shell over a radiator or in your hands to warm the oil a little and make the fondant shell easy to remove. Fill the fondant shell with the sweets, cover with cellophane and tie with ribbon.

Muesli Chocolate Cones

Makes 16

225 g (8 oz) plain cooking chocolate, broken into pieces

2 tablespoons golden syrup

225 g (8 oz) muesli with nuts and fruit

100 g (4 oz) glacé cherries, chopped

Preparation time: 30 minutes, plus setting
Storage time: 2 weeks, in an airtight container

1. Place the chocolate and golden syrup in a bowl over a pan of hot water.
2. When the chocolate has melted, remove the bowl from the pan and stir in the muesli and glacé cherries, mixing thoroughly.
3. Make 16 cones of greaseproof paper from an 18 cm (7 inch) square of paper (see page 4).
4. Pack the mixture tightly into the cones and chill in the refrigerator. Meanwhile, make 16 more cones from coloured paper or fabric. (The fabric cones are also shown on page 92.)
5. Remove the greaseproof paper and drop the cones into the coloured paper or fabric cones. Wrap in cellophane and tie with a ribbon.

Lemon Creams

Makes approximately 16

25 g (1 oz) butter

1 tablespoon milk

grated rind of 1 lemon

2 tablespoons lemon juice

450 g (1 lb) icing sugar, sifted

yellow food colouring

100 g (4 oz) cooking chocolate, to decorate

Preparation time: 40 minutes, plus 24 hours' drying
Cooking time: 6 minutes
Storage time: 3 weeks, in an airtight container

1. Place the butter, milk, lemon rind and juice in a pan and heat gently until the butter has melted. Do not allow the mixture to boil.
2. Cool and, when cold, gradually work in the icing sugar with a wooden spoon.
3. Knead until smooth on a surface dusted with icing sugar. Roll out to a thickness of 5 mm (1/4 inch). Cut into shapes using a small heart-shaped biscuit or pastry cutter.
4. Transfer the shapes to a tray covered with greaseproof paper and leave to set for 24 hours.
5. To decorate, break the chocolate into pieces and place in a basin over a pan of hot water until melted.
6. Pour the chocolate into a greaseproof piping bag (see page 4), cut off the end and drizzle the chocolate over the lemon creams. Leave to set for 1 hour.
7. Pack into boxes, tins or jars. Tie with ribbon and label.

Muesli chocolate cones; Lemon creams

Easter Egg Monsters

Preparation time: 1 hour, plus drying
Storage time: 2 weeks, in a box or covered with paper

Makes 3

225 g (8 oz) almond paste

100 g (4 oz) plain chocolate, melted

3 Easter eggs of any size

green food colouring

3 cherry halves, washed and dried

75 g (3 oz) icing sugar

25 g (1 oz) cocoa powder

40 g (1½ oz) butter, softened

1 tablespoon milk

2 small packets chocolate buttons

2 currants

50 g (2 oz) ready-made fondant icing

25 g (1 oz) blanched almonds, cut into pieces

2 whole cherries

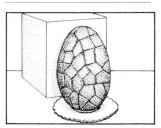

Propping up the egg while it dries on the marzipan base

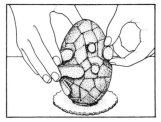

Attaching the shapes to the egg with melted chocolate

Pictured, from the top: Monster Jaws, Monster Frog, Monster Hedgehog

1. On a surface dusted with icing sugar, roll the almond paste to a thickness of 5 mm (¼ inch). Cut out 3 rounds using a 7½ cm (3 inch) fluted pastry cutter.
2. Place a teaspoon of melted chocolate in the centre of each round and stand 2 Easter eggs on their ends in the centre. Position the remaining egg on its side. (The eggs may need supporting with a tin or packet.) Leave to dry for 3 hours.
3. To make the 'Monster Frog', colour the remaining almond paste green, then roll out on a surface dusted with icing sugar and cut out 2 web-shaped arms and a mouth (see the photograph on the right).
4. Shape the remaining almond paste into 2 rounds for eyes and small rounds to stick over the Easter egg 'body'.
5. Spread a little melted chocolate on all the almond paste shapes and attach to one of the Easter eggs on its side: place the eyes on top, the arms at the side, the mouth in the middle and the small green rounds all over the egg. With a little melted chocolate attach 2 cherry halves to the eyes.
6. To make the 'Monster Hedgehog', sift the icing sugar with the cocoa powder and place in a bowl with the butter and milk. Beat with a wooden spoon until smooth.
7. Spoon the icing into a piping bag fitted with a rose nozzle, and pipe rosettes of icing over the other egg on its side, leaving one end clear for the face. Press the chocolate buttons into the icing to form the hedgehog's spines.
8. Pipe a rosette of icing at the 'head' of the egg and attach a cherry half for the snout. Add 2 currants for the eyes, attaching them with a little of the icing.
9. For the 'Monster Jaws', reserve 2 blobs of the fondant icing for the eyes and roll out the rest on a surface dusted with cornflour. Roll into a thin sausage and form into a mouth shape.
10. Brush the mouth with a little melted chocolate and attach to the remaining egg (see the photograph).
11. Stick pieces of almond into the icing to represent teeth and, with the 2 blobs of icing, attach 2 cherries for the eyes.
12. Pack the 'Monsters' in boxes.

Easter Nests

Preparation time: 40 minutes
Cooking time: 15-20 minutes
Oven: 190°C, 375°F, Gas Mark 5
Storage time: 1 week, in an airtight container

Makes 12

65 g (2 1/2 oz) self-raising flour
1/2 teaspoon baking powder
165 g (5 1/2 oz) hard margarine, softened
1/2 tablespoon coffee essence
50 g (2 oz) caster sugar
1 egg, beaten
75 g (3 oz) icing sugar
25 g (1 oz) cocoa powder
1 tablespoon milk
6 large chocolate flakes
48 chocolate mini Easter egg sweets

1. Sift the flour with the baking powder. Place in a bowl with 50 g (2 oz) of the softened margarine, the coffee essence, sugar and egg. Beat with a wooden spoon until the mixture is light and fluffy.
2. Divide the mixture between 12 greased bun tins and bake in a preheated oven for 15-20 minutes until golden brown. Turn out on to a wire rack and leave to cool.
3. To decorate, sift the icing sugar with the cocoa powder and place in a small bowl with the remaining margarine. Stir in the milk and beat with a wooden spoon for 2-3 minutes until light and fluffy.
4. Using a palette knife, spread the icing over the top and sides of each cake.
5. Break the chocolate flake into small strands and press into the icing, overlapping the strands to form a nest and leaving a space in the centre of each cake. Drop 4 mini eggs in each 'nest'.
6. Pack in boxes or tins.

Easter Chicks

Makes 6

1 × 275g (10oz) packet white bread mix

1 egg, beaten

6 almonds, skinned and split in two

6 currants

6 eggs, in their shells

food colourings

Preparation time: 30 minutes, plus rising
Cooking time: 10-15 minutes, plus 5 minutes for the eggs
Oven: 230°C, 450°F, Gas Mark 8
Storage time: Eat on the same day

1. Make up the bread mix according to the packet instructions, and knead on a lightly floured surface for 5 minutes. Divide the dough into 6.
2. To make a chick, take one piece of dough and remove 1/8 for the head. Roll both portions into balls. Make a hole in the large piece of dough so that it looks like a doughnut.
3. Place the dough ring on a greased baking sheet. Attach the small ball of dough with a little beaten egg to form the head. Insert 2 pieces of almond for the beak and press in a currant for an eye.
4. Make up the remaining dough in the same way.
5. Cover with a greased polythene bag and leave to rise in a warm place until double in size.
6. Boil the eggs for 5 minutes, remove from the heat and allow to cool.
7. Place an egg in the space in the middle of each chick. Brush the dough with beaten egg and bake near the top of the oven for 10-15 minutes until golden.
8. When the chicks have cooled, paint a pretty design on the egg shell with the food colourings.
9. Wrap in cling film or cellophane and put in a straw basket.

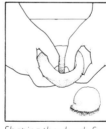

Shaping the dough for the head and body

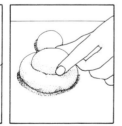

Attaching the head and positioning the egg

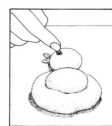

Adding the beak and currant eye

Painting a design on the egg

Makes one 18 cm (7 inch) cake

175 g (6 oz) butter
175 g (6 oz) dark brown sugar
3 eggs, beaten
225 g (8 oz) plain flour
1 teaspoon mixed spice
1 teaspoon ground ginger
1 teaspoon ground nutmeg
225 g (8 oz) mixed dried fruit
100 g (4 oz) glacé cherries, quartered
25 g (1 oz) mixed nuts, chopped
1 tablespoon brandy or milk

To decorate:

1 egg white, beaten
1 bunch violets and freesias
50 g (2 oz) caster sugar
1 tablespoon apricot jam, warmed and sieved
100 g (4 oz) almond paste
50 g (2 oz) icing sugar, sifted
1 tablespoon warm water

Preparation time: 40 minutes, plus drying
Cooking time: 2-2½ hours
Oven: 160°C, 325°F, Gas Mark 3
Storage time: 3 weeks, in an airtight container

1. Grease and line an 18 cm (7 inch) round cake tin.
2. Place the butter and sugar in a bowl and beat with a wooden spoon until creamy and fluffy. Gradually beat in the eggs a little at a time.
3. Sift the flour with the mixed spice, ground ginger and ground nutmeg and fold into the mixture.
4. Stir in the remaining ingredients and place in the prepared tin. Bake in a preheated oven for 2-2½ hours. Leave in the tin to cool.
5. To decorate, put the egg white in a small basin and, using a small, clean, sterilized paint brush, brush the violets and freesias with a little egg white on both sides of the petals. Dip in the sugar and leave to dry for 3 hours.
6. Brush the top of the cake with the warm apricot jam. Roll out the almond paste and place on top of the cake. Flute the edges between thumb and fingers.
7. Blend the icing sugar with enough water to make a smooth paste and pour on top of the cake. Smooth into a circle with the back of a hot metal spoon.
8. Arrange the sugared flowers around the top of the cake and tie a ribbon around the sides.
9. Place in a box or wrap in cellophane.

Fills three 85 ml (3 fl oz) pots

2 × 50 g (2 oz) tins anchovies, drained and chopped
175 g (6 oz) butter, softened
6 green olives, chopped
1 tablespoon lemon juice
¼ teaspoon black pepper

Preparation time: 15 minutes
Storage time: 2 weeks, covered, in the refrigerator

1. Place the anchovies, 100 g (4 oz) butter, olives, lemon juice and pepper in a small bowl. Pound with a potato masher or the end of a rolling pin until well mixed.
2. Pack into sterilized containers (see page 3). Melt the remaining butter and pour over the relish. Leave to set in the refrigerator for 1 hour. Seal and label.
3. Give a jar of the relish as a present with a packet of water biscuits.

Pumpkin Pie

Preparation time: 40 minutes, plus chilling
Cooking time: 1 ¼ hours
Oven: 200°C, 400°F, Gas Mark 6; then 180°C, 350°F, Gas Mark 4
Storage time: 1 week, covered, in the refrigerator

Makes one 20 cm (8 inch) pie

Shortcrust pastry:

225 g (8 oz) plain flour, sifted
50 g (2 oz) margarine
50 g (2 oz) lard
2 tablespoons water
1 tablespoon milk

Filling:

150 g (5 oz) chopped walnuts
1 × 425 g (15 oz) can pumpkin purée
100 g (4 oz) brown sugar
3 tablespoons golden syrup
150 ml (¼ pint) milk
3 eggs, beaten
1 ½ teaspoons ground ginger
1 ½ teaspoons ground cinnamon
1 teaspoon ground nutmeg
grated rind of 2 oranges

1. Place the flour in a bowl and rub in the margarine and lard until the mixture resembles fine breadcrumbs.
2. Add enough of the water to give a firm dough. Gently knead until smooth on a floured surface and chill, covered with greaseproof paper, for 30 minutes.
3. Roll out the pastry on a floured surface and line a pretty 20 cm (8 inch) pie dish. Trim the edge of the pie plate.
4. Roll out the pastry trimmings and cut out small crescents using a tiny cutter. Brush the pastry lip with milk and attach the pastry crescents. Brush the crescents with milk.
5. Fill the centre of the pastry case with greaseproof paper and baking beans and bake 'blind' in a preheated oven for 15 minutes. Lower the oven temperature.
6. Reserve 25 g (1 oz) of the chopped walnuts. Mix all the filling ingredients together. Pour into the pastry case and bake in the oven for 1 hour until the filling has set.
7. Allow to cool, sprinkle with the reserved chopped walnuts and wrap in cling film or cellophane. Tie with ribbon and label.

CHAPTER THREE

Special Occasions

Celebrate those happy or once-in-a-lifetime occasions with a specially designed edible gift to amaze and delight those you love. There are lots of ideas for birthday gifts and ingenious creations such as the 'L-Plate Card' to mark the achievement of passing a driving test and the 'Desert Island Cake' which provides the perfect way to wish someone all the best on their retirement.

Jigsaw Fudge

Makes approximately 750 g (1 ½ lb)
450 g (1 lb) sugar
50 g (2 oz) butter
150 ml (¼ pint) milk
150 ml (¼ pint) evaporated milk
¼ teaspoon almond essence (optional)
To decorate:
100 g (4 oz) almond paste
orange and pink food colourings
1 teaspoon cornflour
1 teaspoon apricot jam, sieved

Preparation time: 1 hour, plus setting and drying
Cooking time: 50 minutes
Storage time: 1-2 weeks, in an airtight container

1. Grease and line an 18 cm (7 inch) square tin.
2. Place the sugar, butter, milk and evaporated milk in a pan and heat gently, stirring with a metal spoon until the sugar has dissolved.
3. Bring to the boil and, stirring occasionally, boil gently until the temperature reaches 115°C/238°F or when a small amount dropped into cold water forms a soft ball.
4. Remove from the heat, stir in the almond essence, if using, and beat the mixture until it becomes thick and 'grainy'.
5. Pour the mixture into the prepared tin and leave to set for about 4 hours. When set, turn out of the tin in one piece.
6. To decorate, colour the almond paste then roll it out thinly on a surface dusted with cornflour.
7. Cut the almond paste into shapes using metal cutters or cardboard shapes to form a flower, picture, someone's name or just a pattern (see the photograph above).
8. Brush the top of the fudge with the sieved apricot jam. Assemble the almond paste shapes in the chosen pattern on top of the fudge. Cut round the shapes and through the fudge. Leave to dry for about 6 hours.
9. Arrange the completed 'picture' in a box, or jumble the fudge pieces in a glass jar or tin. Tie with ribbon and label.

Birthday Gift Tags

Makes 8

rice paper

225 g (8 oz) plain chocolate, broken into pieces

25 g (1 oz) butter

1 egg

550 g (1¼ lb) icing sugar, sifted

grated rind of 1 orange

6 tablespoons condensed milk

coloured string or ribbon

green food colouring

yellow sugar-coated chocolate sweets

Preparation time: 1¾ hours, plus drying
Storage time: 2-3 weeks, in an airtight container

1. Line the base of a 20 cm (8 inch) loose-bottomed square tin with the rice paper.
2. Place the chocolate and butter in a large bowl over a pan of hot water and heat gently until the chocolate has melted. Add the egg and whisk until the mixture is thick and creamy.
3. Mix in 450 g (1 lb) of the icing sugar, the orange rind and condensed milk. Remove from the heat and continue mixing until it becomes very thick.
4. Press the mixture into the prepared tin and leave for 6 hours to harden. Remove from the tin and cut into eight 5 × 10 cm (2 × 4 inch) oblongs. F
5. Make a hole in one corner of each tag with a clean knitting needle and thread with coloured string or ribbon.
6. Place the remaining icing sugar in a small bowl and add enough water to form a thick smooth paste. Colour it green with the food colouring. Pour into a greaseproof paper piping bag (see page 4), snip off the end and pipe a name or short message, allocating one letter per sweet. Stick the sweets to the top of the tag with a little icing. Alternatively, stick the sweets around the edge of the tag and pipe a message in the centre.
7. Wrap the tags in cellophane or cling film and pack carefully in a box.
F Wrap in foil and freeze for up to 6 months. Thaw overnight, uncovered.

Grandma's Birthday Card

Makes 1 card

Knitting needles:

1 tablespoon cornflour

100g (4oz) fondant icing
(page 4)

1 tablespoon icing sugar, sifted

1 teaspoon water

Shortbread base:

100g (4oz) plain flour

50g (2oz) cornflour

100g (4oz) butter, softened

50g (2oz) caster sugar

grated rind of 1 lemon

To decorate:

length of red ribbon

175g (6oz) icing sugar, sifted

1-2 tablespoons warm water

red and green food colourings

Preparation time: 2 hours, plus 8 days' drying
Cooking time: 45 minutes
Oven: 160°C, 325°F, Gas Mark 3
Storage time: 1 week, in an airtight container

1. First, make the knitting needles: dust a rolling pin or your fingers and the working surface with cornflour to prevent the fondant icing from sticking. Divide the fondant icing into 3 portions.
2. Take 2 portions of the fondant, remove a small piece from each and shape into 2 'buttons' to form the ends of the needles.
3. Roll the remaining fondant into two 15 cm (6 inch) 'pencil' shapes with points at one end. These form the 'shafts' of the knitting needles.
4. Divide the last portion of fondant in half and roll one half into a ball shape. Roll the remainder into an oblong 5 × 6cm (2 × 2½ inches). Lift the long end and concertina slightly.
5. Place all the fondant shapes on a board covered with greaseproof paper dusted with cornflour. Cover with greaseproof paper or paper towels and leave to dry in a warm place for 4 days.
6. After 4 days, blend the icing sugar with a little water to make an edible 'glue'. Stick the 'buttons' of fondant on to the ends of the needles and leave for a further 3 days to dry.
7. When the knitting needles are dry, make the shortbread base. Sift together the flour and cornflour in a mixing bowl. Rub the butter into the dry ingredients until the mixture resembles fine bread-crumbs. Stir in the sugar and lemon rind.
8. Knead and press the mixture into a smooth, silky ball. Press into a 20 cm (8 inch) fluted flan ring.
9. Bake in a preheated oven for 45 minutes until golden. Remove from the oven and immediately score the shortbread into 8 portions, without actually cutting through it. Cut 2 small holes near the left-hand edge of the shortbread (see the photograph top right). Leave to cool on a wire tray.
10. To assemble, place the shortbread on a small silver board. Thread the red ribbon through the holes on the side and tie in a bow.
11. Blend the icing sugar with sufficient warm water to form a stiff, smooth icing.

Attaching the fondant needles and ball of wool to the base

Piping icing to form the 'knitting' and ball of wool

12. Slightly cross the 'knitting needles' and attach them to the shortbread base with a little glacé icing. Prop the 'needles' with a small roll of paper towel until the icing has dried.

13. Place the fondant ball on one side of the 'needles' and the oblong 'concertina' piece of fondant in front. Secure both with a little icing.

14. Colour 2 tablespoons of the remaining icing red and the rest green. Pipe green stitches on to the needles and horizontal rows beneath the needles and across the oblong of fondant. Next, pipe strings of continuous loops like little 'u's' between all the horizontal lines. This will form the 'knitting'. To make it look realistic make the 'stitches' irregular. Finally, pipe strands of wool round and over the ball of fondant and take a thread from the ball to the needles.

15. Place the red glacé icing in a fine piping tube and write a greeting on the card. Leave to dry for a day.

16. Pack into a cardboard box or overwrap in cellophane. Tie with ribbon and label.

Racing Track Cake

Makes 1 cake to serve 16-20

Cake:

350 g (12 oz) self-raising flour

2 teaspoons baking powder

350 g (12 oz) caster sugar

350 g (12 oz) butter, softened

6 eggs

grated rind of 1 orange

pink and yellow food colourings

To decorate:

2 tablespoons apricot jam,
warmed and sieved

2 egg whites

350 g (12 oz) icing sugar, sifted

6 tablespoons water

pinch of salt

2 teaspoons lemon juice

small toy cars for racing track

Preparation time: 2 hours
Cooking time: 40 minutes
Oven: 180°C, 350°F, Gas Mark 4
Storage times: Eat the same day it is iced

This cake is also an obvious choice for an eighth birthday celebration. It can be decorated according to the child's interests or hobbies.

1. Grease and flour two 1.75 litre (3 pint) ring mould tins.
2. Sift the flour with the baking powder and place all the cake ingredients, except the food colourings, in a bowl. Beat with a wooden spoon until thoroughly combined.
3. Divide the mixture into 3 portions. Leave one portion plain, add a few drops of pink food colouring to the second portion and yellow to the third. Mix the colourings into the cake mixtures with a wooden spoon.
4. Fill the prepared tins with the cake mixture, alternating the colours in each tin. Swirl a skewer through the cake mixture to mix the colours together thoroughly.
5. Bake in a preheated oven for 40 minutes until golden brown. Turn the cakes out of the tins and leave to cool on a wire tray. F
6. To decorate, cut a thin slice off each cake vertically. Brush the cut edges with the apricot jam and push the cakes together on a silver board to form the shape of an '8'.
7. Place the egg whites, icing sugar, water, salt and lemon juice in a large bowl over a pan of boiling water. Whisk for 10 minutes with a rotary whisk or 5 minutes with an electric whisk until the mixture thickens and stands in peaks. Remove from the heat and continue whisking until the mixture is cold.
8. Swirl the icing immediately over the cake with a palette knife.
9. Smooth part of the icing to form a track around both parts of the cake. Place model cars on the track.
10. Pack the cake in a box and tie with ribbon.
F Wrap the cakes in foil and freeze for up to 3 months. Thaw overnight wrapped in foil.

Gingerbread House

Makes 1

200 g (7 oz) golden syrup

100 g (4 oz) butter

90 g (3½ oz) demerara sugar

2 teaspoons ground ginger

1 teaspoon ground cinnamon

2 teaspoons bicarbonate of soda

1 egg, beaten

475 g (1 lb 2 oz) plain flour, sifted

To decorate:

2 egg whites, beaten

450 g (1 lb) icing sugar, sifted

1 silver board

food colourings of your choice

100 g (4 oz) coconut

assorted sweets (jellies, chocolate buttons, etc)

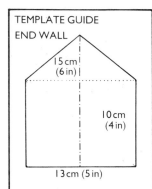

TEMPLATE GUIDE
END WALL

15 cm (6 in)

10 cm (4 in)

13 cm (5 in)

SIDE WALL
18 cm (7 in) × 10 cm (4 in)
ROOF
20 cm (8 in) × 10 cm (4 in)
DOOR
2½ cm (1 inch) × 1 cm (½ inch)

Preparation time: 2 hours, plus drying
Cooking time: 1 hour – 1 hour 15 minutes
Oven: 160°C, 325°F, Gas Mark 3
Storage time: 1-2 weeks, in a tin

1. Cut out cardboard patterns from cereal packets, following the diagrams given below left for the roof, door, end and side walls.
2. Put the golden syrup, butter, demerara sugar, ginger and cinnamon in a large saucepan. Heat gently until the sugar and butter have melted. Bring to the boil and remove from the heat.
3. Stir in the bicarbonate of soda and pour the mixture into a large bowl. Beat in the egg and sifted flour with a wooden spoon, then knead to a smooth dough in the bowl.
4. Turn on to a lightly floured surface and roll out to a thickness of 5 mm (¼ inch). Using the cardboard patterns as a guide, cut out a roof, door, side and end wall. Reserve the trimmings. Place the dough shapes on greased baking sheets and bake in a preheated oven for 20-25 minutes. Leave the shapes for 2 minutes, then carefully remove them from the baking sheets with a fish slice and place on a wire tray. Allow to cool completely.
5. Gather the trimmings together, re-roll and cut out another roof, side and end wall. Bake as for the first batch.
6. Re-roll the final trimmings and use biscuit cutters to cut out 2 small figures and 2 trees. Cut 4 small oblongs of dough to use as the bases for the figures and trees. Place the shapes on greased baking sheets and bake for 10-15 minutes. Remove to a wire tray and leave to cool.
7. To assemble the house, place the beaten egg whites in a medium-sized basin and beat in the sifted icing sugar a little at a time until the mixture is smooth, shiny and white.
8. Spread a little of the icing on all edges of the side and end walls. Stand the pieces on a silver board and press together like a box (see the pictures on page 45). Allow to dry for 2 hours.
9. Spread a little of the icing on the top edges of the walls, underneath the roof 2½ cm (1 inch) in from the edge and along the top join of the roof. Carefully position the roof and press into place. Hold in position for a few minutes until the icing begins to set.

Assembling the sides of the house

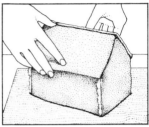

Attaching the roof to the walls

10. Attach the door to one end wall with a little icing. Spread the small oblongs of gingerbread with icing and attach the gingerbread people and trees, supporting until the icing has set.

11. To decorate, place the coconut in a small bowl, add a few drops of green food colouring and mix thoroughly. Spread a thin layer of icing over the cake board and cover with the green coconut. Pipe squares for the windows on the sides of the house.

12. Colour teaspoons of icing and pipe curtains at the windows, and decorate the door (see the photograph below). Pipe swirls of icing around the edge of the board and, if wished, press in the desired number of candles.

13. Pipe small blobs of icing on some sweets and press on to the roof and sides of the house in a pattern (see the photograph below).

14. Using coloured icing, pipe features and clothes on the figures and decorate the trees with icing. Stick sweets together with a little icing to form a chimney on the roof (see the photograph below).

15. Allow to dry for at least 2 hours and pack into a box.

Makes 1 cake to serve 12

3 eggs

100 g (4 oz) caster sugar

100 g (4 oz) plain flour

1 tablespoon hot water

4 tablespoons pineapple jam, warmed

500 g (1 1/4 lb) almond paste

yellow food colouring

3 tablespoons apricot jam, warmed and sieved

175 g (6 oz) sweets, dolly mixtures, jellies

100 g (4 oz) icing sugar, sifted

1 tablespoon orange juice

red and blue food colouring (optional)

ribbon

candles (optional)

Preparation time: 1 1/2 hours
Cooking time: 7-9 minutes
Oven: 220°C, 425°F, Gas Mark 7
Storage time: 4 days, in an airtight container

1. Grease and line a 33 × 23 cm (13 × 9 inch) Swiss roll tin.
2. Place the eggs and sugar in a large bowl, stand over a pan of hot water on a gentle heat and whisk until the mixture is very thick and foamy. Remove from the heat and whisk until cool. (If using an electric mixer, no heat is needed.)
3. Sift half the flour over the mixture and fold in carefully with a metal spoon. Repeat with the remaining flour and stir in the hot water.
4. Pour the mixture into the prepared tin and bake immediately in a preheated oven for 7-9 minutes until golden brown.
5. Cover a damp tea towel with a sheet of greaseproof paper sprinkled with sugar. Turn the cake out on to the sugared paper and remove the lining paper. Spread the warm cake with the pineapple jam and roll up from one shorter side using the sugared paper to help. Cool on a wire tray.
6. To decorate, knead a few drops of yellow colouring into the almond paste. Turn on to a surface dusted with icing sugar and roll to an oblong wide enough to fit round the roll and 15 cm (6 inches) longer.
7. Brush the Swiss roll with apricot jam and wrap the almond paste around it. Stand on a cake board. Pinch the almond paste at each end of the Swiss roll and flute the edges to form a cracker.
8. Cut the cake in the middle and pull the 2 pieces apart slightly. Fill the gap with sweets.
9. Place the sifted icing sugar in a small bowl and add the water, a little at a time, beating with a wooden spoon, until the icing is smooth and thick. Colour the icing with food colourings and pipe a name, message or pattern on top of the cracker.
10. Tie a ribbon at each end of the cracker and, if wished, push in the appropriate number of candles. Place in a box or tin.

Birthday cracker; Thank you biscuits (recipe on page 48)

Thank You Biscuits

Makes the letters THANK YOU

100 g (4 oz) butter, softened
150 g (5 oz) caster sugar
1 egg yolk
225 g (8 oz) plain flour
¼ teaspoon ground mixed spice
grated rind of 1 orange

To decorate:

50 g (2 oz) icing sugar, sifted
1 - 1 ½ tablespoons orange juice
cherries and angelica

(Pictured on page 46.)

Preparation time: 30 minutes
Cooking time: 25 minutes
Oven: 180°C, 350°F, Gas Mark 4
Storage time: 3 weeks, in an airtight container

1. Place the butter and sugar in a bowl and cream with a wooden spoon until light and fluffy. Add the egg yolk and beat in thoroughly.
2. Sift the flour with the mixed spice and stir into the mixture with the orange rind. Mix to a firm dough. Knead lightly on a floured surface until smooth.
3. Divide the dough into 8 portions. Shape each piece into a long roll and, with your fingers, mould into individual letters to make up the words THANK YOU. Place on a greased baking sheet, allowing room to spread and bake in a preheated oven for 25 minutes until golden brown. Allow to cool slightly before removing from the baking sheet.
4. To decorate, blend the icing sugar with enough orange juice to form a thick, smooth icing.
5. Use blobs of glacé icing to attach sweets or cherries and pieces of angelica to the biscuits. Leave to set.
6. Pack into an airtight container, then tie with ribbon and label.

Rolling pieces of dough into sausage shapes and modelling to form letters

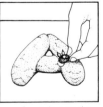

Attaching cherries and pieces of angelica to the biscuits with a little icing

L' Plate Card

Makes I card

175 g (6 oz) almond paste

red food colouring

100 g (4 oz) icing sugar, sifted, plus extra, for dusting

water

25 g (1 oz) cooking chocolate, broken into pieces

length of string

Preparation time: I hour, plus 3 days' drying
Storage time: 6 months, in an airtight container

1. Roll two-thirds of the almond paste on a surface lightly dusted with sifted icing sugar to a 13 cm (4 inch) square.
2. Carefully lift with a fish slice or a palette knife on to a piece of card. Cut a small hole in the top corners, cover with a clean cloth and leave to dry overnight.
3. Knead a few drops of red food colouring into the remaining almond paste and roll out on a surface lightly dusted with icing sugar. Cut out 2 strips: one measuring 7½ × 1 cm (3 × 1 inch), and the other measuring 5 × 1 cm (2 × 1 inch). Place on a piece of greaseproof paper, cover with a clean cloth and leave to dry overnight.
4. Place the icing sugar in a bowl and, beating with a wooden spoon, add enough water to give a smooth, flowing icing.
5. Place a wire rack on a tray and lift the almond paste square on to the wire rack. Pour the glacé icing over the square and leave to dry for 24 hours. Pour the remaining glacé icing from the tray into a small dish, and cover with cling film.
6. With a little of the glacé icing, attach the almond paste strips to the card to form an 'L'.
7. Place the chocolate in a small basin over a pan of hot water and heat until the chocolate has melted. Pour into a greaseproof piping bag (see page 4), snip off the end and pipe a thick irregular zig-zag line diagonally across the cake to give the appearance of the card having been torn in two.
8. Leave to dry overnight, thread string through the holes and place in a box.

Desert Island Cake

Makes one 18 cm (7 inch) cake

Cake:

225 g (8oz) plain flour

3 teaspoons mixed spice

½ teaspoon baking powder

175 g (6 oz) butter, softened

175 g (6oz) dark brown sugar

3 eggs

225 g (8 oz) mixed dried fruit

100 g (4 oz) hazelnuts, chopped

1 tablespoon port

Almond paste:

225 g (8 oz) ground almonds

100 g (4 oz) icing sugar, sifted

100 g (4 oz) caster sugar

1 teaspoon lemon juice

2 drops almond essence

1 egg, beaten

75 g (3 oz) apricot jam, warmed and sieved

Royal icing:

2 egg whites

450 g (1 lb) icing sugar, sifted

1 teaspoon glycerine

blue food colouring

To decorate:

25 g (1 oz) desiccated coconut

green food colouring

175 g (6 oz) fondant icing (page 4)

blue, green, black, pink and yellow food colourings

Preparation time: 3 hours, plus 2-3 days' drying
Cooking time: 2-2½ hours
Oven: 160°C, 325°F, Gas Mark 3
Storage time: 2 months, in a box

This cake is perfect for a retirement party.

1. Grease and line an 18 cm (7 inch) round cake tin.
2. Sift the flour with the mixed spice and baking powder and place all the cake ingredients in a bowl and beat with a wooden spoon for 4-5 minutes or with an electric mixer for 2-3 minutes until thoroughly combined.
3. Turn the mixture into the prepared tin. Smooth the top with the back of a wet metal spoon and make a small hollow in the centre.
4. Bake in a preheated oven for 2-2½ hours. The cake is cooked when a skewer pushed into the middle comes out clean. Leave in the tin for 30 minutes before turning out on to a wire tray. Remove the paper lining and leave to cool.
5. To make the almond paste, place the ground almonds, icing sugar and caster sugar in a bowl and mix together with a wooden spoon. Add the lemon juice, almond essence and enough beaten egg to form a stiff paste.
6. Gather the mixture together with the fingers and knead into a ball. Turn on to a surface dusted with icing sugar, knead until smooth and roll out thinly. Cut out a circle to fit the top of the cake and a strip to fit the sides.
7. Stand the cake on a silver board and brush the top and sides with the warmed apricot jam. Cover the top of the cake with the circle of almond paste and press the strip around the sides. Smooth the joins with a knife and leave to dry for 24 hours.
8. To make the royal icing, place the egg whites in a large bowl and beat with a fork until frothy. Add the icing sugar a little at a time, beating thoroughly with a wooden spoon, until the icing is very stiff and white. Stir in the glycerine.
9. Place half of the icing in a small bowl and mix with a few drops of blue food colouring. Reserve 3 tablespoons of white icing in a bowl and cover with cling film. Swirl the white and blue icing over

Swirling the icing over the cake to form waves

Modelling the man and the beach towel

the sides and top edge of the cake to resemble waves. Spread a very thin coating of icing over the top of the cake.

10. To decorate, put the coconut in a teacup, add 2 drops of green colouring and a few drops of water. Mix thoroughly and sprinkle on top of the cake to represent grass.

11. On a surface dusted with cornflour knead the fondant icing until smooth, then divide into 4 portions.

12. Shape one piece into 2 balls for a head and body and sausage shapes for 2 arms and legs. Moisten the joins with water and press the pieces together.

13. Take another piece of icing and roll into a 3 × 7½ cm (1½ × 3 inch) oblong to make a towel. Slash each end to form a fringe.

14. Divide a third piece of fondant into 7 portions and model 6 cones of varying sizes, cut slits in the tops and open them

Recipe continues on page 52.

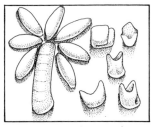

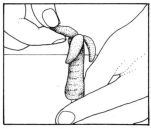

Modelling the palm tree, the book and the sharks

Assembling the palm tree: attaching the leaves to the trunk with a little icing

Desert Island Cake *continued.*

out a little to form the heads of sharks. Model the seventh piece into a book.

15. Finally, roll out the fourth piece and cut diamonds to form the leaves of a palm tree; model the remainder into a trunk.

16. Using a fish slice lift the shapes carefully on to non-stick silicone paper, cover with a cloth and leave to dry for 3 hours in a warm place.

17. Place the man on the towel on the top of the cake. Attach the sharks to the waves with a little of the reserved icing. Place the book next to the man. Stand the palm tree at the back of the cake and attach the leaves with a little icing. Support the tree with cocktail sticks or rolls of paper towels until dry. Leave to dry overnight.

18. Use a clean fine paintbrush and the food colourings to paint the modelled items. Leave to dry for 12 hours. Pack the cake into a box or tin.

*Bon
Voyage
Gâteau*

Makes 1 cake to serve 8

Cake:

50 g (2 oz) butter, softened

100 g (4 oz) caster sugar

2 eggs

100 g (4 oz) self-raising flour, sifted

1/4 teaspoon almond essence

Caramel:

175 g (6 oz) sugar

6 tablespoons water

Filling:

50 g (2 oz) sultanas

2 tablespoons Amaretto (almond liqueur) or orange juice

25 g (1 oz) ground almonds

3 tablespoons nutty chocolate spread

To decorate:

300 ml (1/2 pint) whipping or double cream, whipped

175 g (6 oz) almonds, chopped and toasted

Preparation time: 1 1/2 hours
Cooking time: 10-12 minutes
Oven: 200°C, 400°F, Gas Mark 6
Storage time: Eat on the same day

1. Grease and line a 28 × 18 cm (11 × 7 inch) Swiss roll tin.
2. Place all the cake ingredients in a mixing bowl and beat together with a wooden spoon for 2-3 minutes until thoroughly combined.
3. Pour the mixture into the prepared tin and bake in a preheated oven for 10-12 minutes until golden brown.
4. Turn out on to a wire tray, remove the lining paper and leave to cool. Cut the cake into four 6 × 18 cm (2 × 7 inch) pieces.
5. To make the caramel, put the sugar and water in a heavy-based saucepan and heat slowly, stirring with a metal spoon, until the sugar has dissolved. Bring to the boil and continue boiling until the syrup becomes a golden brown.
6. Pour some of the caramel over the top of one piece of cake and the remainder on to a sheet of greaseproof paper.
7. To make the filling, place the sultanas and liqueur or orange juice in a small pan and heat gently until the sultanas have absorbed the liquid. Leave to cool completely.
8. Mix together the sultanas, almonds and chocolate spread in a small bowl. Spread the filling on the 3 remaining pieces of cake and sandwich together. Finish off with the caramel-topped cake.
9. Lift the cake carefully on to a board and coat the sides of the cake with two-thirds of the whipped double cream. Press the toasted almonds on to the sides of the cake with a palette knife.
10. Place the remaining cream in a piping bag fitted with a star nozzle and pipe rosettes around the base and top edge of the cake. Pipe 'Bon Voyage' over the caramel topping.
11. Peel the greaseproof paper away from the sheet of caramel and break into pieces with the end of a rolling pin. Push the cracked caramel pieces into the rosettes of cream.
12. Pack the cake into a box, tin or airtight container. Tie with ribbon and attach a label.

Christening Bootee

Makes 1 cake to serve 12

Cake:

450g (1 lb) plain flour

3 teaspoons baking powder

350g (12 oz) butter, softened

350g (12 oz) caster sugar

6 eggs

1/2 teaspoon almond essence

To decorate:

6 tablespoons apricot jam, warmed and sieved

750g (1 1/2 lb) fondant icing (page 4)

pink or blue food colouring (optional)

satin ribbon

100g (4 oz) sugared almonds

Preparation time: 2 hours
Cooking time: 50-60 minutes
Oven: 160°C, 325°F, Gas Mark 3
Storage time: 1 week, in an airtight container

1. Grease and flour four 10 cm (4 inch) round cake tins.
2. Sift the flour with the baking powder, place all the cake ingredients in a bowl and beat with a wooden spoon for 3-4 minutes until thoroughly combined.
3. Divide the mixture between the 4 tins and bake in a preheated oven for 50-60 minutes until golden brown. Turn the cakes out on to a wire tray and cool.
4. To decorate, put 3 of the cakes on top of each other, sandwiching with the apricot jam, and place on a cake board.
5. Cut the fourth cake in half vertically. With the curved sides up, sandwich the two halves with apricot jam and place in front of the cake on the board.
6. If liked, colour the fondant icing pink for a girl or blue for a boy. Roll the icing on a surface dusted with cornflour. Cut out one piece to cover the 'foot' and the remainder to cover the 'leg', leaving extra at the top to form a collar.
7. Brush the cake with apricot jam, then wrap the fondant around the cake and, with fingers dipped in cornflour, smooth the icing.
8. With a knife, score a line down the front of the leg, making sure you do not cut through to the cake. Make small lines on either side of the central line to represent buttonholes.
9. Neaten the edges of the fondant with metal crimpers or a fork. Make 2 holes in the icing which forms the collar, thread through a length of ribbon and tie into a bow. Fill the top with sugared almonds.
10. Pack the cake carefully in a box.

CHAPTER FOUR

Presents for Keeps

A home-made delicacy can make a much appreciated gift, so when making your preserves, hoard away an extra batch which you can package prettily and give when presents are needed.

Tipsy Marmalade

Makes approximately 4½ kg (10 lb)

1¼ kg (3lb) Seville oranges

1 grapefruit

8 tablespoons lemon juice

3.5 litres (6 pints) water

2¾ kg (6lb) preserving sugar

150 ml (¼ pint) Irish whiskey

Preparation time: 1 hour
Cooking time: 40 minutes
Storage time: 1 year

1. Squeeze the juice from the oranges and grapefruit and pour into a large preserving pan. Tie the pips in a piece of muslin and add to the juice in the pan. Add the lemon juice.
2. Thinly slice the orange and grapefruit peel and add to the pan.
3. Pour over the water, bring to the boil and simmer for 1½ hours until the peel has softened. Remove the muslin bag of pips and squeeze the juice into the pan by pressing the bag between 2 wooden spoons.
4. Add the sugar and heat gently, stirring with a wooden spoon until the sugar has dissolved. Pour in the whiskey.
5. Bring to the boil and boil rapidly for about 20 minutes until setting point is reached, 104°C/220°F on a sugar thermometer, or when a little of the marmalade poured on to a cold saucer and cooled begins to wrinkle when you push it with your finger. Remove the scum from the top of the marmalade.
6. Allow to cool slightly and pour into hot, sterilized jars (see page 3). Cover with waxed discs and cellophane secured with elastic bands and label.
7. Tie ribbon around the neck of the jars or cover with a frill or circle of fabric tied with string or ribbon.

Garlic Cheese

Makes one 225 g (8 oz) cheese

1.75 litres (3 pints) milk

2 tablespoons lemon juice

2 tablespoons vinegar

2 cloves garlic, crushed

salt

freshly ground black pepper

To garnish:

3 tablespoons nibbed almonds, or 3 tablespoons black peppercorns, or 100 g (4 oz) vine leaves and a length of raffia

Preparation time: 1 hour, plus draining
Cooking time: 15 minutes
Storage time: 1 week, covered, in the refrigerator

1. Sterilize a sieve, a piece of muslin and a bowl in boiling water for 10 minutes before beginning to make the cheese.
2. In a pan bring the milk to the boil, then add the lemon juice and vinegar. Leave to stand for 15 minutes to produce curds and whey.
3. Line the sieve with muslin, rest over the bowl and pour in the curds and whey.
4. Draw up the corners of the muslin and tie securely. Suspend with a bowl underneath to catch the whey and leave for 3 hours.
5. Turn the curds into a bowl and beat in the crushed garlic. Add salt and black pepper to taste. Discard the whey.
6. Pat the cheese into a round, triangle or log shape and coat with either the nibbed almonds or peppercorns.
7. Alternatively, line a yogurt or dessert container with vine leaves. Fill with the cheese, fold over the leaves and weigh down for a few hours. Turn out and tie with a length of raffia.
8. Wrap in greaseproof paper or muslin and store in the refrigerator.

Damson cheese; Pineapple butter; Tarragon vinegar

Tarragon Vinegar

Makes approximately 2.25 litres (4 pints)

1.2 litres (2 pints) white wine vinegar
1.2 litres (2 pints) red wine vinegar
4 handfuls tarragon leaves
4 attractive sprigs tarragon

Preparation time: 30 minutes, plus 2 weeks' standing
Cooking time: 5 minutes
Storage time: 1 year

1. Pour the vinegars into separate pans and bring to the boil. Remove from the heat and allow to cool slightly.
2. Place a handful of tarragon leaves into each of 4 warm, sterilized 600 ml (1 pint) bottles (see page 3). Pour over the vinegar and stand the bottles in a light, warm room for 2 weeks.
3. Strain into clean, sterilized bottles. Discard the tarragon leaves and add a fresh sprig of tarragon to each bottle.
4. Seal with plastic-coated lids, corks or a screw-top, and label.
5. Attach a tag giving instructions for the use of the vinegar as a salad dressing and tie ribbon around the neck.

Preparation time: 30 minutes
Cooking time: 1 hour
Storage time: 3-6 months

This 'butter' can be used as a cake filling, or served with scones or cakes. It also makes a delicious sauce for ice cream.

Makes approximately 750 g (1½ lb)

450 g (1 lb) pineapple, diced
225 g (8 oz) diced apple
2 tablespoons lemon juice
150 ml (¼ pint) water
sugar (see right)

1. Place the pineapple, apple, lemon juice and water in a pan, Cover and cook gently, stirring occasionally, for approximately 30-40 minutes until the fruit has softened.
2. Sieve or liquidize and weigh the purée. Return to the pan with 350 g (12 oz) sugar to every 450 g (1 lb) purée. Heat gently, stirring with a wooden spoon, until the sugar has dissolved.
3. Bring to the boil and cook for approximately 15-20 minutes until very thick and creamy.
4. Allow to cool slightly, then pour into hot, sterilized jars (see page 3). Cover with waxed discs and cellophane secured with elastic bands and label.
5. Tie a length of ribbon around the neck of the jars or cover with a frill or circle of fabric tied with string or ribbon.

Preparation time: 40 minutes
Cooking time: 50 minutes
Storage time: 1 year

This 'cheese' is halfway between a jam and a jelly. It can be made in wide-necked jars or small moulds, then turned out and served in slices with cold meat. Or simply spread it on cake or scones.

Makes approximately 2¼ kg (5 lb)

2¾ kg (6 lb) damsons, stalks removed and washed
300 ml (½ pint) water
sugar (see right)

1. Place the damsons and water in a large pan. Bring to the boil and simmer until the fruit has softened, about 15 minutes.
2. Sieve and weigh the pulp. Return to a clean pan with 450 g (1 lb) sugar to each 450 g (1 lb) fruit pulp.
3. Heat gently, stirring with a wooden spoon, until the sugar has dissolved. Continue to cook, stirring, until the purée is very thick and a spoon drawn across the base of the pan leaves a clean line through the mixture.
4. Pour into hot, sterilized jars which have been oiled (see page 3) or into small moulds. Cover with waxed discs and cellophane, then label and decorate the jars with ribbon.

Boozy Fruits

Makes two 750 g (1½ lb) jars

100 g (4 oz) blanched almonds
450 g (1 lb) dried apricots
350 g (12 oz) dried pears
100 g crystallized pineapple, chopped
1 × 70 cl bottle sweet white wine

Preparation time: 15 minutes, plus maturing
Storage time: 1 year

The fruit and syrup can be eaten after 2 months straight from the bottle or simmered in a little orange juice for 15 minutes. Serve with cream, ice-cream or pancakes.

1. Mix the nuts and fruits together.
2. Pack into 2 sterilized wide-necked jars (see page 3). Pour over the wine and seal tightly.
3. Tie a length of lace or net around the neck of the jar and label with instructions for use, as described above.

Raspberry and Almond Conserve

Makes approximately 1¾ kg (4 lb)

1¾ kg (4 lb) raspberries, hulled
1¾ kg (4 lb) sugar
4 tablespoons lemon juice
100 g (4 oz) almonds, blanched
6 tablespoons Cointreau

Preparation time: 1 hour, plus standing overnight
Cooking time: 30-40 minutes
Storage time: 3 months

1. Place the raspberries and sugar in alternate layers in a large bowl. Cover and leave overnight to extract the juices and firm the fruit.
2. Strain the juices into a pan and reserve the fruit. Add the sugar to the juices in the pan and heat gently, stirring occasionally, until all the sugar has dissolved. Stir in the lemon juice.
3. Bring to the boil and simmer until the syrup has reduced by half. Add the raspberries and simmer for 10-15 minutes until the raspberries are cooked, but still firm. Stir in the almonds and Cointreau.
4. Allow to cool completely before pouring int cold sterilized jars (see page 3). Cover with waxed discs and cellophane secured with elastic bands and attach labels.
5. Tie ribbon around the neck of the jars, or cover with a frill or circle of fabric tied with string or ribbon.

Clockwise from the front: Boozy fruits; Grapefruit and lime curd; Raspberry and almond conserve

Grapefruit and Lime Curd

Makes approximately 1 kg (2 lb)

grated rind of 1 grapefruit

8 tablespoons grapefruit juice

grated rind of 1 lime

4 tablespoons lime juice

350 g (12 oz) sugar

4 eggs, beaten

Preparation time: 10 minutes
Cooking time: approximately 50 minutes
Storage time: 1 month

1. Place all the ingredients in a bowl over a pan of hot water.
2. Heat gently until the sugar has dissolved and continue until the mixture thickens, stirring occasionally.
3. The curd is ready when it is thick and coats the back of a wooden spoon, about 30 minutes.
4. Pour the curd into sterilized jars or bottles (see page 3). Cover, seal and label the jars and decorate with lengths of ribbon.

Preparation time: 30 minutes every 2 weeks throughout the summer
Storage time: 8 months

Begin making this German preserve at the beginning of the summer with strawberries and continue throughout' the fruit season, adding each fruit as it becomes available. It will be ready in time to eat at Christmas.

Makes as much or as little as you want. All the summer fruits as they come into season

450 g (1 lb) fruit to 225 g (8 oz) sugar

white rum with a high alchohol content (see right)

1. To start the rumtopf, wash and dry 450 g (1 lb) strawberries. Place in a large glass jar, earthenware crock or a special rumtopf jar.
2. Add 225 g (8 oz) sugar and pour over 600 ml (1 pint) white rum. Stir and cover.
3. Keep in a cool place and every two weeks add more fruit and sugar in the proportions of half the weight of sugar to the fruit weight. Pour over enough rum to keep the liquid level just above the level of the fruit.
4. When the jars are full, cover, seal and decorate with ribbon and label.

CHAPTER FIVE

Surprise Presents

It is an unexpected treat to receive a gift instead of only a card, especially if you can eat it too! This chapter features lots of home-made goodies which can be given on any occasion.

Cake Decorations

Makes 1 box of decorations

*100 g (4 oz) fondant icing
(page 4)*

*red, yellow and orange food
colourings*

2 tablespoons cornflour

1 egg white

225 g (8 oz) icing sugar, sifted

*50 g (2 oz) sugar, or coloured
sugar crystals*

*50 g (2 oz) plain chocolate,
broken into pieces*

Preparation time: 4 hours,
plus drying (several days,
for roses and bells)
Storage time: Roses and
Bells: 1 year;
Chocolate shapes:
3 months

Choose a pretty box and, with pieces of
card, divide into 3 sections. Fill each
section with the decorations which can be
used on cakes, puddings, or biscuits.

Roses
1. Knead a few drops of red food
colouring into the fondant icing, or leave
it plain (see step 5).
2. To make a petal, place a small ball of
fondant, the size of a pea, in the palm of
one hand and flatten with a finger of the
other hand. (Dip your fingers into
cornflour to prevent the fondant from
sticking.) Wrap the petal around the end
of a knitting needle.
3. Make more petals in the same way
and wrap them loosely around the first
petal, still on the knitting needle. Roll the
edges of the outer petals to give them a
realistic look.
4. When the roses are the size you wish,
gently remove from the needle and place
on a plate covered with greaseproof
paper. Leave to dry for 1 week.
5. If the fondant icing has been left plain,
you could paint red or yellow food
colouring just on the edges of the petals.
Iced bells
1. Place the egg white in a bowl and beat
with a fork until frothy. Gradually add the
icing sugar, beating with a wooden spoon,
until the icing is thick and smooth.
2. Place two-thirds of the icing in a
greaseproof piping bag (see page 4) and
snip off the end. Pipe blobs of icing the
size of a 10p piece on to a sheet of non-
stick silicone paper. Pipe smaller blobs on
top of the larger ones. Leave to dry
overnight in a warm room.
3. Carefully lift each shape from the
paper and, with the end of a spoon,
scoop out and discard the soft icing from
the centre.

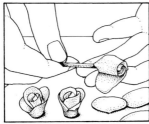

*Wrapping fondant icing around
a knitting needle to form rose
petals*

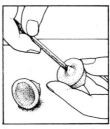

*Scooping out the soft
icing from the bells*

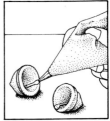

*Piping the clapper in
the bells*

4. Put the remaining icing into a piping bag, snip off the end and pipe the clapper in the bell. To do this, turn the bells on their sides and pipe a straight line inside from the centre to the rim, finishing with a blob. Leave to dry for several days.

Chocolate shapes

1. Place the chocolate in a small bowl over a basin of hot water and heat until the chocolate has melted.

2. Draw 5 cm (2 inch) circles and squares on a sheet of non-stick silicone paper. Turn the paper over and place on a tray.

3. Pour the melted chocolate into a piping bag fitted with a small writing tube. Following the drawn lines, pipe the outlines of the circles and squares. Pipe diagonal or zig-zag lines across the shapes and leave to dry overnight, then very carefully peel the shapes away from the greaseproof paper.

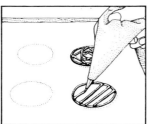

Piping chocolate shapes within outlines on silicone paper

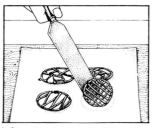

Lifting the shapes carefully with a palette knife

Honey Toffee

Makes approximately 225 g (8 oz)

75 g (3 oz) clear honey

25 g (1 oz) butter

150 g (5 oz) sugar

5 tablespoons water

Preparation time: 10 minutes
Cooking time: 50 minutes
Storage time: 2 weeks, in an airtight container

1. Place the honey, butter, sugar in a heavy-based pan. Heat very slowly, stirring with a metal spoon until the sugar has dissolved.
2. Stop stirring and bring to the boil. Boil until the temperature reaches 151°C/304°F or when a little syrup poured into cold water forms brittle threads which snap easily.
3. Remove from the heat and pour into a greased 18 cm (7 inch) square tin. Mark into squares and, when set, snap the toffee into individual pieces.
4. Wrap the pieces of toffee in cellophane or cling film and pack into tins or jars. Tie with coloured string or ribbon and label.
Variation:
Nut toffee: Stir 100 g (4 oz) mixed nuts into the toffee before pouring into the tin.

Rum Truffles

Makes 20

225 g (8 oz) chocolate cake crumbs

25 g (1 oz) ground almonds

25 g (1 oz) chocolate, melted

1 tablespoon crystallized ginger, finely chopped (optional)

about 3 tablespoons rum

To decorate:

25 g (1 oz) chopped almonds, toasted

25 g (1 oz) chocolate vermicelli

Preparation time: 40 minutes
Storage time: 3 weeks, in an airtight container

1. Place all the truffle ingredients in a bowl and mix thoroughly to form a stiff mixture. Add a little more rum or a little milk if the mixture is too dry.
2. Divide the mixture into 20 portions and roll into balls. Toss 10 of the truffles in the chopped almonds until completely coated and the remainder in the chocolate vermicelli. F
3. Place each truffle in a petit-four case and pack them into boxes. Tie with ribbon and label.
F Freeze for up to 3 months. Thaw overnight at room temperature.

Top: Honey toffee; Bottom: Rum truffles

Swimming Pool Cake

Makes one 18 cm (7 inch) cake

225 g (8 oz) butter, softened

175 g (6 oz) caster sugar

3 eggs, beaten

225 g (8 oz) plain flour

1½ teaspoons baking powder

225 g (8 oz) glacé cherries, washed, dried and chopped

2 tablespoons milk

225 g (8 oz) icing sugar, sifted

175 g (6 oz) desiccated coconut

2 tablespoons apricot jam, warmed and sieved

175 g (6 oz) almond paste

3 × 18 cm (7 inch) thin strips liquorice

blue, pink and brown food colourings

150 ml (¼ pint) pineapple juice

1 tablespoon gelatine

Preparation time: 3 hours, plus drying and setting
Cooking time: 1½ hours
Oven: 160°C, 325°F, Gas Mark 3
Storage time: 1 week, in an airtight container

1. Grease and line an 18 cm (7 inch) square cake tin.
2. Place 175 g (6 oz) of the butter in a bowl with the caster sugar and beat with a wooden spoon until light and fluffy. Gradually add the egg, beating well between each addition.
3. Sift the flour with the baking powder and fold into the mixture with a metal spoon. Stir in the cherries.
4. Put the mixture into the prepared tin and bake in a preheated oven for 1½ hours until golden brown. Turn out on to a wire tray, remove the paper lining and cool.
5. To make the butter icing, put the remaining butter in a bowl with the milk and icing sugar and beat with a wooden spoon until light and fluffy. Spread the icing over the sides of the cake.
6. Pour the coconut on to a plate and press each side of the cake into the coconut.
7. On a surface dusted with icing sugar, roll 75 g (3 oz) of the almond paste to a 20 cm (8 inch) square. Stand the cake on a board and brush the top with apricot jam. Place the almond paste square on top of the cake and press down. Roll the edges of the almond paste to form a small collar around the top of the cake.
8. To decorate, place the 3 liquorice strips at intervals on top of the cake, pressing into the almond paste a little, to form 4 swimming lanes.
9. Brush the almond paste with blue food colouring diluted with a little water. Leave to dry for 2 hours in a warm place.
10. Colour the remaining almond paste pink with a little food colouring and model 4 small balls for heads and 16 thin sausage shapes for arms and legs, flattened at one end for hands and feet.
11. Place a 'body' in each lane, with the head, arms and legs sticking out of the water (the main body is out of sight beneath the water!). Paint features and hair on the heads with food colouring. Leave to dry for 1 hour.
12. Put the pineapple juice in a small pan, sprinkle over the gelatine and heat gently until the gelatine has dissolved. Leave to cool. When the jelly is almost setting, carefully pour it around the figures on top of the cake and smooth the jelly to cover the cake. Leave to set.
13. Place the cake carefully in a box.

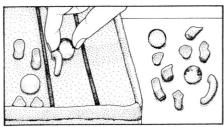

Modelling almond paste shapes for heads, arms and feet

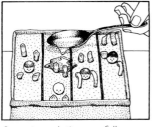

Spooning gelatine carefully around the positioned bodies

Get Well Soon Card

Makes I card

I egg white

I bunch freesias or violets

I tablespoon sugar

---

100 g (4 oz) butter, softened

---

75 g (3 oz) caster sugar

---

75 g (3 oz) plain flour, sifted

I tablespoon golden syrup

---

2 tablespoons condensed milk

---

50 g (2 oz) plain or milk cooking
chocolate, broken into pieces

---

50 g (2 oz) icing sugar, sifted

Preparation time: I hour, plus drying
Cooking time: 15-20 minutes
Oven: 180°C, 350°F, Gas Mark 4
Storage time: Without the flowers, I week in an airtight container. With the flowers, eat within I or 2 days.

I. Line a 15 cm (6 inch) square cake tin with greaseproof paper.
2. Put the egg white in a small dish and beat with a fork until frothy.
3. Remove the clean petals from the flowers and brush both sides with egg white or dip into the egg white and shake off the excess. Dip the petals in the sugar and, when coated, leave to dry on greaseproof paper in a warm place for about 3 hours.
4. To make the card, place 50 g (2 oz) of the butter and 25 g (1 oz) of caster sugar in a bowl and cream together with a wooden spoon until light and fluffy. Gradually work in the flour and knead with the fingers to form a stiff dough. Press the dough into the prepared tin and bake in a preheated oven for 15-20 minutes until golden brown. Leave in the tin to cool completely, then remove carefully.
5. Place the remaining butter and sugar,

golden syrup and condensed milk in a heavy-based pan. Heat gently, stirring with a wooden spoon, until the sugar has dissolved. Bring to the boil and continue boiling for 5-10 minutes until golden and a small amount dropped into cold water forms a soft ball (118°C/245°F). Pour the syrup over the shortbread base and leave to cool.

6. Place the chocolate in a bowl over a pan of hot water and heat gently until the chocolate has melted. Pour the melted chocolate over the caramel and spread with a knife to smooth. Leave to set for at least 1 hour.

7. To decorate, stand the card on a piece of thin card or a small cake board. Place the icing sugar in a small bowl and mix with a wooden spoon, adding a few drops of water at a time, until the icing is thick and smooth.

8. Attach the sugared flowers around the edge of the card with a little icing. Pour the remaining icing into a greaseproof paper bag (see page 4) and snip off the end of the bag. Pipe 'Get well soon' on the card and leave to dry for about 1 hour.

9. Place the card in a box, then tie with ribbon and label.

The freesias and violets can be eaten, if wished. If you prefer, you can use silk flowers or almond paste shapes instead of fresh flowers (see also Simnel cake, page 34 and Sparkling fruit tarts, page 84).

Variation:
White chocolate can be used instead of plain or milk chocolate.

Nutty Teabread

Preparation time: 40 minutes, plus cooling
Cooking time: 1-1¼ hours
Oven: 180°C, 350°F Gas Mark 4
Storage time: 2 weeks, in an airtight container

Makes one 1 kg (2 lb) loaf

225 g (8 oz) self-raising flour

½ teaspoon baking powder

¼ teaspoon salt

¼ teaspoon ground mixed spice

100 g (4 oz) dates, chopped

100 g (4 oz) crunchy peanut butter

100 g (4 oz) caster sugar

50 g (2 oz) butter, softened

2 eggs

grated rind of 1 large orange

4 tablespoons orange juice

about 2 tablespoons milk

To decorate:

100 g (4 oz) caster sugar

65 ml (2½ fl oz) water

175 g (6 oz) whole mixed nuts

1. Grease and bottom-line a 1 kg (2 lb) loaf tin.
2. Sift the flour with baking powder, salt and mixed spice. Place the mixture with all the cake ingredients, except the milk, in a bowl and beat with a wooden spoon for 2-3 minutes until thoroughly combined. Add enough of the milk to give a dropping consistency.
3. Place the mixture in the prepared loaf tin and bake in a preheated oven for 1-1¼ hours. Turn out on to a wire rack and leave to cool. F
4. To decorate, put the sugar and water in a pan over a low heat and stir with a metal spoon until the sugar has dissolved.
5. Bring to the boil and cook without stirring until the liquid has reduced by half and begins to turn a golden colour. A small amount dropped into water will harden. Quickly stir in the whole nuts and pour the mixture on top of the teabread. Allow to cool completely.
6. Replace the teabread in the loaf tin if it is to form part of the present. If not, place the loaf on a cake board. In both cases, overwrap in cellophane, tie with ribbon and label.
F Freeze for up to 4 months. Thaw for 4 hours at room temperature. Decorate.

Swiss Nut Tart

Makes one 18 cm (7 inch) tart

Pastry:

225 g (8oz) plain flour, sifted

50 g (2 oz) white fat, softened

50 g (2 oz) hard margarine, softened

water

1 egg, beaten

Filling:

15 g (½ oz) butter

225 g (8 oz) sugar

175 g (6 oz) walnuts, roughly chopped

150 ml (¼ pint) double cream

Preparation time: 30 minutes, plus chilling
Cooking time: 30-40 minutes
Oven: 200°C, 400°F, Gas Mark 6
Storage time: 1 week, in an airtight container

1. In a mixing bowl rub the white fat and margarine into the flour until the mixture resembles fine breadcrumbs. Add enough water to form a firm dough, cutting through the mix with a palette knife until it begins to form a ball in the bowl.

2. Turn on to a lightly floured surface and knead gently until smooth. Cover and chill for 30 minutes.

3. Roll out two-thirds of the pastry on a lightly floured surface and line an 18 cm (7 inch) loose-bottomed deep flan tin. The pastry should hang over the edge of the flan tin. Brush the base of the pastry case with beaten egg.

4. To make the filling, place the butter and sugar in a heavy-based saucepan and heat very gently, stirring with a metal spoon, until the sugar has dissolved. Continue to heat, without stirring, until the colour becomes a pale golden brown.

5. Remove from the heat and add the walnuts and cream. Stir thoroughly with a spatula and return to the heat, stirring constantly, until almost at boiling point. Leave to cool, then pour the walnut mix into the flan case.

6. Roll the remaining pastry on a lightly floured surface to fit the top of the flan. Brush the edge of the pastry in the flan case with a little beaten egg and cover with the pastry lid. With a sharp knife trim away the excess pastry and pinch the edge of the pastry between thumb and finger. Reserve the trimmings.

7. Re-roll the trimmings and cut out small fluted circles using a small cutter. Brush the pastry tart with beaten egg and arrange the pastry shapes around the top. Brush the shapes with a little beaten egg. Bake in a preheated oven for 30-40 minutes until golden brown. Turn out and cool on a wire tray.

8. Return the flan to the tin as it is part of the present and stand on a thin silver board. Cover with cling film and tie with a length of ribbon.

(Pictured on page 74.)

Glacé Fruit Cake

Makes one 20 cm (8 inch) cake

275 g (10 oz) plain flour

1 teaspoon baking powder

½ teaspoon mixed spice

½ teaspoon ground cinnamon

350 g (12 oz) glacé cherries, washed and dried

225 g (8 oz) blanched almonds

100 g (4 oz) angelica, washed and dried

100 g (4 oz) crystallized ginger, washed and dried

100 g (4 oz) crystallized pineapple, washed and dried

100 g (4 oz) sultanas

225 g (8 oz) butter, softened

150 g (5 oz) caster sugar

4 eggs, beaten

2 tablespoons milk

4 tablespoons white or dark rum

2 tablespoons apricot jam, warmed and sieved

Caramel glaze:

175 g (6 oz) sugar

6 tablespoons water

Preparation time: 1 hour, plus standing
Cooking time: approximately 3-3½ hours
Oven: 140°C, 275°F, Gas Mark 1
Storage time: 6 weeks, wrapped in foil or in an airtight container

1. Grease and line a 20 cm (8 inch) round cake tin.
2. In a small bowl sift together the flour, baking powder, mixed spice and ground cinnamon.
3. Chop 175 g (6 oz) of the glacé cherries into quarters, roughly chop 100 g (4 oz) of the blanched almonds and 50 g (2 oz) each of angelica, crystallized ginger and pineapple. Mix these together with the sultanas in a bowl.
4. Place the butter and sugar in another large bowl and beat with a wooden spoon until light and fluffy. Stir in the beaten egg, a little at a time, adding a little of the flour and spice if the mixture begins to separate.
5. With a large metal spoon fold in the flour and spices. Stir in the milk, 2 tablespoons of the rum and the fruit and nut mixture and mix thoroughly. Turn into the prepared tin, press the mixture down well and make a small hollow in the centre.
6. Bake in the middle of the preheated oven for 3-3½ hours until the cake is golden brown. After 3 hours test to see if the cake is cooked by pushing a warm skewer into the middle; if the skewer comes out clean, the cake is cooked.

Leave in the tin for 15 minutes before turning on to a wire tray. Remove the lining paper and leave to cool.

7. Make small holes in the top of the cake with a skewer and pour over the remaining rum. [F]

8. To decorate, stand the cake on a board and brush the top with the warmed apricot jam. Halve the remaining cherries, slice the remaining almonds in half and slice the remaining angelica, ginger and pineapple. Arrange in a pattern on top of the cake.

9. Place the sugar and water in a small heavy-based saucepan and heat very gently, stirring with a metal spoon, until the sugar has dissolved. Increase the heat and bring to the boil without stirring, then continue boiling until pale golden brown.

10. Leave for a minute to cool slightly, then carefully pour over the fruit on top of the cake. Take care not to touch the caramel with your fingers. Leave the cake to cool for 15 minutes.

11. Tie a ribbon around the cake and place in a box or airtight container and tie with ribbon.

[F] Wrap in foil and freeze for up to 3 months. Thaw wrapped in foil for 4 hours at room temperature, then decorate.

Variations:
Substitute 1 teaspoon of ground ginger in place of the mixed spice and cinnamon.

Alter the proportions of fruit according to your taste – make an all pineapple cake, for example.

Serving suggestion:
This cake is delicious served with wedges of Caerphilly cheese.

*Left: Swiss nut tart (recipe on page 73); **Right:** Glacé fruit cake*

Chocolate Torte

Makes one 18 cm (7 inch) cake

50 g (2 oz) cooking chocolate, broken into pieces

20 roses leaves, washed

175 g (6 oz) self-raising flour

1 1/2 teaspoons baking powder

1 1/2 tablespoons cocoa powder

2 tablespoons hot water

3 eggs

175 g (6 oz) butter, softened

175 g (6 oz) caster sugar

To decorate:

100 g (4 oz) plain chocolate, broken into pieces

50 g (2 oz) butter

100 g (4 oz) icing sugar, sifted

2 tablespoons orange liqueur or milk (non-alcoholic alternative)

50 g (2 oz) nougat, finely chopped

100 g (4 oz) peanut brittle, crushed

300 ml (1/2 pint) double or whipping cream, whipped

Preparation time: 1 1/2 hours
Cooking time: 40-45 minutes
Oven: 160°C, 325°F, Gas Mark 3
Storage time: 2 days, in a box or airtight container.

1. Grease and bottom-line two 18 cm (7 inch) sandwich tins.
2. Place the cooking chocolate in a small basin over a pan of hot water and heat until melted. Dip one side of the rose leaves in the chocolate and leave to dry for 3 hours on non-stick silicone paper.
3. Sift the flour with the baking powder. Blend the cocoa powder with the hot water and leave to cool.
4. Place all the cake ingredients in a large mixing bowl and beat with a wooden spoon for 2-3 minutes until thoroughly combined.
5. Pour the mixture into the prepared cake tins and bake in a preheated oven for 40-45 minutes until the cakes spring back when pressed. Turn out on to a wire tray, remove the lining paper and leave to cool.

Gingerbread fish (recipe on page 78); Chocolate torte

6. To make the filling, place the chocolate and butter in a small bowl over a pan of hot water and heat until melted. Remove from the heat and stir in the icing sugar and liqueur or milk. Add a little milk if the filling is stiff. Fold in the nougat and half the peanut brittle.

7. Cut each cake in half horizontally and sandwich all 4 layers together with the chocolate filling. Stand the cake on a board and spread two-thirds of the whipped cream over the top and sides of the cake. Swirl with a knife or neaten with an icing comb.

8. Fill a piping bag fitted with a rose nozzle with the remaining cream and pipe rosettes around the base and top edge of the cake.

9. Carefully peel the chocolate away from the rose leaves and decorate the cake with the chocolate leaves, veins uppermost. Sprinkle the remaining peanut brittle in the centre of the cake.

10. Place carefully in a box or airtight container.

Gingerbread Fish

Preparation time: 1¾ hours
Cooking time: 1½ hours
Oven: 160°C, 325°F, Gas Mark 3
Storage time: Gingerbread: 3 weeks
Decorated cakes: 1 week

Makes 9

---

175 g (6 oz) margarine

---

100 g (4 oz) black treacle

---

175 g (6 oz) demerara sugar

---

275 g (10 oz) plain flour

¾ teaspoon bicarbonate of soda

---

2 teaspoons ground ginger

1½ teaspoons ground cinnamon

---

75 g (3 oz) almonds, blanched
and finely chopped

---

2 tablespoons milk

---

3 eggs, beaten

To decorate:

---

225 g (8 oz) icing sugar, sifted

---

75 g (3 oz) butter or margarine,
softened

---

2 tablespoons milk

---

225 g (8 oz) chocolate buttons
covered in hundreds and
thousands

---

9 small jellies

---

9 tiny pieces of angelica

---

9 ice cream wafers

---

1. Grease and line a 23 cm (9 inch) square cake tin.
2. Put the margarine, treacle and sugar in a small pan and heat gently until the sugar has dissolved. Leave to cool.
3. Sift the flour, bicarbonate of soda, ground ginger and cinnamon into a large bowl. Stir in the almonds and raisins.
4. Pour over the cooled treacle and the milk, add the eggs, then beat with a wooden spoon for 2-3 minutes until thoroughly combined.
5. Pour the mixture into the prepared tin and bake in a preheated oven for 1½ hours. Turn out on to a wire tray, remove the paper lining and leave to cool. When cold, cut into nine 7½ cm (3 inch) circles. F
6. To decorate, place the icing sugar, butter or margarine and milk in a basin and beat with a wooden spoon until light and fluffy.
7. Coat the top and sides of each cake with the icing. Leaving a small area clear for the face, arrange the chocolate buttons overlapping on the cake to form the scales.
8. Use one jelly for the eye and a small piece of angelica for the mouth. Cut the wafers into triangles, 4 for each cake. Push the wafers into the icing to form 2 fins and a tail.
9. Using a fish slice, carefully place each cake on a small doily and then on a small cake board or circle of thick card. Pack the 'fish' into boxes or a tin, tie with ribbon and label.
F Open-freeze the gingerbread circles, pack in a single layer in an airtight container and freeze for up to 6 months. Thaw for 3 hours at room temperature.

Variations:
Instead of the chocolate buttons covered in hundreds and thousands, use white chocolate buttons or crumbled chocolate flakes.

(Pictured on page 76.)

CHAPTER SIX

Bazaars and Fêtes

Are you short of ideas for money-raising events? Would you like to see people flocking to your stall, attracted by something unusual? Look no further than the following recipes!

Sage Jelly

Makes approximately 1 kg (2 lb)

1 kg (2 lb) cooking apples, washed and chopped

900 ml (1 ½ pints) water

300 ml (½ pint) wine vinegar

4 tablespoons lemon juice

2 handfuls sage leaves

sugar (see right)

Preparation time: 15 minutes, plus standing overnight
Cooking time: 1 ½ hours
Storage time: 1 year

1. Place the apples in a large pan. Pour over the water, wine vinegar, lemon juice and half of the sage leaves.
2. Bring to the boil, cover and simmer for 30 minutes until the apples are pulpy.
3. Pour into a jelly bag or a muslin-lined colander positioned over a bowl and leave to drip overnight. (Do not squeeze the bag otherwise the jelly will be cloudy.)
4. Measure the juice, then pour into a large pan with 450 g (1 lb) sugar for every 600 ml (1 pint) juice.
5. Heat gently, stirring until the sugar has dissolved. Bring to the boil and boil rapidly until setting point is reached, 104°C/220°F, or when a small amount dropped on to a cold saucer and cooled slightly begins to wrinkle.
6. Chop the remaining sage and stir into the jelly. Allow to cool slightly and pour into small, hot, sterilized jars (see page 3). Cover and label.
7. Tie ribbon around the neck of the jars or cover with a frill or circle of fabric tied with string or ribbon.

Three-Fruit Jam

Makes approximately 2¼ g (5 lb)

450 g (1 lb) redcurrants

450 g (1 lb) blackcurrants

450 g (1lb) blackberries, washed

grated rind of 1 orange

4 tablespoons orange juice

1 ½ kg (3 ½ lb) preserving sugar

Preparation time: 1 hour
Cooking time: 1 hour
Storage time: 1 year

1. Strip the currants off the stalks by running a fork down each stalk.
2. Place the currants, blackberries, orange rind and juice in a large preserving pan. Heat gently to extract the juice from the fruit, then bring to the boil and simmer for 10-15 minutes until the fruit skins have softened.
3. Add the sugar and heat gently, stirring with a wooden spoon, until the sugar has dissolved.
4. Bring to the boil and boil rapidly until setting point is reached, 104°C/220°F on a sugar thermometer, or when a little of the jam poured on to a cold saucer and cooled begins to wrinkle when pushed with a finger.
5. Remove the scum from the top of the jam, allow to cool slightly and pour into hot, sterilized jars (see page 3). Cover with waxed discs and cellophane secured with elastic bands and label.
6. Tie ribbon around the neck of the jars or cover with a frill or circle of fabric tied with string or ribbon.

Plum Chutney

Makes approximately 2 kg (4½ lb)

1 kg (2 lb) plums, quartered and stoned

225 g (8 oz) onions, chopped

225 g (8 oz) grated cooking apple

225 g (8 oz) sugar

100 g (4 oz) carrot, grated

100 g (4 oz) raisins

100 g (4 oz) sultanas

600 ml (1 pint) malt vinegar

25 g (1 oz) salt

1 teaspoon ground ginger

3 cloves garlic, crushed

2 teaspoons ground allspice

Preparation time: 40 minutes
Cooking time: 1 hour
Storage time: 1 year

Serve this chutney with cheese dishes or cold meats. To make a delicious sauce to accompany kebabs, fish dishes or cooked vegetables, stir 1 tablespoon of the chutney into a carton of plain yogurt.

1. Place all the ingredients in a preserving pan or a large heavy-based pan and heat slowly until the sugar has completely dissolved.
2. Bring to the boil and simmer for approximately 1 hour, stirring occasionally, until the mixture has become very thick.
3. Pour into hot, sterilized pots or jars (see page 3) and cover with plastic-coated lids.
4. Cut out circles of fabric, trim the edges with pinking shears and tie on to the top of the jars with ribbon.

Three-fruit jam; Sage jelly; Plum chutney

Preparation time: 30 minutes
Cooking time: 20-25 minutes
Oven: 190°C, 375°F, Gas Mark 5
Storage time: 2 weeks, in an airtight container

Viennese Whirls

Makes 12

225 g (8 oz) butter
100 g (4 oz) icing sugar, sifted
grated rind of 1 lemon
200 g (7 oz) plain flour
50 g (2 oz) cornflour
2 tablespoons lemon curd
2 tablespoons raspberry jam
2 tablespoons greengage jam

1. Cream together the butter, 75 g (3 oz) of the icing sugar and the lemon rind until light and fluffy.
2. Sift together the flour and cornflour and stir into the butter mixture.
3. Put the mixture into a piping bag fitted with a star nozzle and pipe into 12 paper cake cases, swirling round the inside of the paper case.
4. Place the cakes on a baking sheet and bake near the top of a preheated oven for 20-25 minutes until golden. Leave to cool. F
5. When cold sift the remaining icing sugar over the top and place a small blob of lemon curd or jam in the middle of each.
6. Pack in layers between sheets of greaseproof paper in tins or boxes. Tie with string or ribbon and label.
F Freeze for up to 3 months. Thaw for 3 hours at room temperature.

Fudge-topped Gingerbread

Makes 16 squares

175 g (6 oz) brown sugar
100 g (4 oz) margarine, softened
200 g (7 oz) golden syrup
50 g (2 oz) black treacle
400 g (14 oz) plain flour
1 ½ teaspoons baking powder
½ teaspoon bicarbonate of soda
2 teaspoons ground ginger
1 egg
150 ml (¼ pint) milk

Fudge icing:

225 g (8 oz) icing sugar, sifted
50 g (2 oz) margarine, softened
3 tablespoons milk
100 g (4 oz) chopped walnuts

Preparation time: 40 minutes
Cooking time: 1 ½ hours
Oven: 150°C, 300°F, Gas Mark 2
Storage time: 2 weeks, in an airtight container

1. Grease and line a 23 cm (9 inch) square cake tin.
2. Place the sugar, margarine, golden syrup and treacle in a pan. Heat gently, stirring constantly, until the sugar has dissolved. Leave to cool.
3. Sift together the flour, baking powder, bicarbonate of soda and ground ginger.
4. Pour over the cooled syrup and add the egg and milk. Beat until smooth.
5. Pour the mixture into the prepared tin. Bake in a preheated oven for 1 ½ hours. Leave in the tin to cool.
6. To make the fudge icing, place the icing sugar, margarine and milk in a bowl over a pan of hot water and stir until the icing is smooth and glossy.
7. Remove from the heat and allow to cool. When cold, beat until the icing has thickened.
8. Swirl the icing over the top of the gingerbread and sprinkle over the walnuts. Leave to set, then cut into 16 squares.
9. Pack the gingerbread in a tin or box or wrap individual pieces in cellophane.

Sparkling Fruit Tarts

Makes 6

Pastry:

225 g (8 oz) plain flour

1/4 teaspoon ground ginger

50 g (2 oz) white fat, softened

50 g (2 oz) hard margarine, softened

water

Filling:

175 g (6 oz) black and white grapes

1 bunch violets or freesias, stalks removed

1 egg, separated

25 g (1 oz) caster sugar

150 ml (1/4 pint) whipping cream

2 tablespoons lemon curd

Preparation time: 40 minutes, plus chilling
Cooking time: 15 minutes
Oven: 200°C, 400°F, Gas Mark 6
Storage time: Eat on the same day

1. Sift the flour with the ground ginger and rub the white fat and margarine into the flour and ginger until the mixture resembles fine breadcrumbs. Add enough water to form a firm dough, cutting through the mix with a palette knife until it begins to form a ball.
2. Turn the dough on to a lightly floured surface and knead gently until smooth. Cover and chill for 30 minutes.
3. Brush the grapes and flowers with a little egg white using a clean brush, then roll in the sugar and stand on paper towels in a warm place for 30 minutes.
4. Roll the pastry on a lightly floured surface and line six 10 cm (4 inch) fluted flan cases. Place crumpled greaseproof paper in the middle of each case and bake 'blind' in a preheated oven for 12 minutes until golden.
5. Remove the greaseproof paper, brush the inside of the pastry cases with beaten egg yolk, then return to the oven and cook for a further 3 minutes. Turn out and cool on a wire tray.
6. Pour the cream into a small bowl and whisk until thick. Fold in the lemon curd. Divide the cream mixture between the flan cases and top with the sugared grapes and flowers.
7. Place in a box or tin and tie with ribbon.

Coconut Ice

Makes 1 1/2 kg (3 lb) in 4 bars

400 g (14 oz) can condensed milk

500 g (18 oz) icing sugar, sifted

350 g (12 oz) desiccated coconut

few drops pink food colouring

4 long strands of liquorice

Preparation time: 40 minutes, plus standing overnight
Storage time: 1 month, in an airtight container

1. Mix together the condensed milk and the icing sugar in a bowl. With a wooden spoon, stir in the desiccated coconut; the mixture will be very stiff.
2. Line the base of a 20 cm (8 inch) square tin with greaseproof paper and dust with icing sugar. Using your fingers, press half of the mixture into the tin.
3. Add a few drops of pink colouring to the remaining mixture. Knead well and press on top of the white ice in the tin.
4. Leave to set overnight. Cut into 4 bars and tie each with a length of liquorice. Overwrap in cling film or cellophane.

Sugar Mice

Makes 8

450 g (1 lb) icing sugar, sifted

1 egg white, lightly beaten

50 g (2 oz) golden syrup

1-2 teaspoons cornflour, for dusting

1-2 teaspoons icing sugar, for dusting

To decorate:

coloured silver balls

coloured narrow ribbon

Preparation time: 40 minutes, plus 2 days' drying
Storage time: 6 months, in an airtight container

1. Place half of the sugar, the beaten egg white and golden syrup in a bowl. Beat with a wooden spoon until smooth. Gradually add the remaining sugar.
2. Knead on a surface dusted with icing sugar and cornflour. Divide the mixture into 8 portions.
3. To shape a mouse, take one piece of fondant icing and remove a tiny piece for 'ears'.
4. Shape the remaining piece into a ball, flatten and draw out one end to form the head. Press 2 coloured silver balls into the head to form eyes (see the photograph below).
5. Shape the small piece of fondant to make 2 ears. Make small holes in the head where the ears will be and push the base of the ears into the holes to secure.
6. Make a small hole at the end of the mouse and push in a length of coloured ribbon for the tail. Match the ribbon colour to the eyes.
7. Place on and cover with non-stick silicone paper and leave to dry in a warm room for 2 days.
8. Wrap in cellophane paper and tie with string or ribbon.

Toffee Apples

Makes 8

175 g (6 oz) golden syrup

350 g (12 oz) dark brown sugar

25 g (1 oz) butter

150 ml (¼ pint) water

1 teaspoon vinegar

8 eating apples, washed

To decorate:

2 tablespoons sesame seeds

2 tablespoons desiccated coconut

2 tablespoons chopped peanuts

Preparation time: 30 minutes
Cooking time: 30 minutes
Storage time: 1 week, in an airtight container

1. Place the golden syrup, sugar, butter, water and vinegar in a large heavy-based pan over a low heat. Stir with a metal spoon until the sugar has dissolved. Do not allow to boil.
2. Remove the spoon, increase the heat and boil to the soft crack stage, 138°C/280°F, or when a little syrup dropped into iced water forms a hard ball.
3. Remove from the heat, place the base of the pan in cold water, and, when the bubbles have subsided, push the lollipop sticks into the apples and dunk them in the toffee. When thoroughly coated, let the excess toffee fall back into the saucepan.
4. Dip each apple into cold water to set the toffee. Sprinkle each decoration over 2 apples, leaving 2 plain. Stand on greaseproof paper and leave to cool.
5. Wrap each apple in cellophane, twisting it around the lollipop stick, and decorate with ribbon.

Sugar mice; Toffee apples with a variety of coatings

Carrot Cake

Makes one 18 cm (7 inch) cake

75 g (3 oz) self-raising flour

2 teaspoons baking powder

75 g (3 oz) wholewheat flour

175 g (6 oz) butter, softened

175 g (6 oz) caster sugar

50 g (2 oz) walnuts, finely chopped

50 g (2 oz) raisins, chopped

275 g (10 oz) carrots, finely grated

3 eggs

1 tablespoon milk

To decorate:

225 g (8 oz) full fat soft cheese

100 g (4 oz) icing sugar, sifted

rind of 1 lemon

4 tablespoons lemon juice

50 g (2 oz) almond paste

orange food colouring

small piece of angelica

Preparation time: 50 minutes
Cooking time: 50-60 minutes
Oven: 180°C, 350°F, Gas Mark 4
Storage time: 1 week, in an airtight container in the refrigerator

1. Grease and line an 18 cm (7 inch) round cake tin.
2. Sift the flour with the baking powder, then place all the cake ingredients in a large bowl and beat with a wooden spoon for 3-4 minutes until thoroughly combined.
3. Pour into the prepared tin and bake in a preheated oven for 50-60 minutes until golden brown and firm to the touch. Turn out on to a wire tray, remove the lining paper and leave to cool.
4. To decorate, place the cheese, icing sugar, lemon rind and juice in a bowl, and beat with a wooden spoon until smooth.
5. Place the cake on a silver board or plate and coat the sides and top with the icing. Smooth with a palette knife, or swirl with a fork or an icing comb.
6. Knead a few drops of orange food colouring into the almond paste. Divide the paste into 6 portions and mould into carrot shapes. Make small lines across the carrots to make them look realistic.
7. Wash and dry the angelica and cut into 6 small pieces. Push a piece into each end of the carrots, then place the carrots on top of the cake.
8. Pack in a box or tin. Tie with ribbon and label.

Spiced Nuts

Makes 225 g (8 oz)

2 tablespoons oil

1 tablespoon curry powder

1 tablespoon sesame seeds

1 tablespoon black onion seeds

1 teaspoon ground coriander

1/2 teaspoon salt

1/4 teaspoon freshly ground black pepper

225 g (8 oz) mixed nuts

Preparation time: 10 minutes
Cooking time: 10 minutes
Storage time: 3 weeks, in an airtight container

1. Heat the oil in a pan and add the curry powder, sesame and onion seeds and coriander.
2. Cook the spices for 2 minutes, stirring with a wooden spoon.
3. Add salt, pepper and the mixed nuts. Fry gently for 8 minutes.
4. Drain on paper towels. When cold, put into a jar or container. Seal and label.

Spiced nuts; Carrot cake; Nutty cheese breads (recipe on page 90)

Nutty Cheese Breads

Makes two 750 g (1½ lb) loaves

20 g (¾ oz) fresh yeast

15 g (½ oz) brown sugar

450 ml (¾ pint) milk and water mixed in equal proportions, warmed

350 g (12 oz) strong plain white flour

350 g (12 oz) plain wholemeal flour

½ tablespoon salt

75 g (3 oz) strong Cheddar cheese, grated

1 teaspoon powdered mustard

75 g (3 oz) shelled, skinned peanuts, finely chopped

1 egg, beaten

2 tablespoons poppy seeds

Preparation time: 40 minutes, plus proving
Cooking time: 30-40 minutes
Oven: 230°C, 450°F, Gas Mark 8
Storage time: 2 days, in a bread bin

1. Cream together the yeast and sugar in a medium-sized bowl. Stir in the warmed milk and water, mix thoroughly and leave in a warm place until bubbles appear on the surface (about 10 minutes).
2. Place the white and wholemeal flours, salt, grated cheese, mustard and 50 g (2 oz) of the peanuts in a large bowl. Stir until thoroughly mixed.
3. Make a well in the centre of the flour, pour in the frothy yeast mixture and mix together with a palette knife to form a dough. Turn the dough on to a lightly floured surface and knead until smooth.
4. Return the dough to the mixing bowl, cover with a clean cloth or a piece of greased polythene and leave in a warm place until doubled in size (about 1 hour).
5. Turn the risen dough on to a lightly floured surface, knead until smooth and cut in half. Cover with a clean cloth.
6. To make a cottage loaf, take one portion of the dough and cut off one third. Knead both pieces on a lightly floured surface and shape into 2 rounds. Place the large round on a greased baking sheet, brush the top with beaten egg and place the smaller round on top. With the floured handle of a wooden spoon, push down the centre of both rounds to secure them together.
7. For a plaited loaf, take the remaining dough, cut in half and knead both pieces on a lightly floured surface until smooth. Roll each piece into a strip 40 cm (16 inches) long. On a clean surface arrange the 2 strips of dough in a cross. Take each end of the strip underneath and cross them over in the centre. Repeat with the other strip of dough. Cross over each strip of dough alternately until all the dough is used. Pinch together the ends and place the plait on its side on a greased baking sheet.
8. Cover both the cottage and plaited loaves with a clean cloth and leave in a warm place until doubled in size (about 30 minutes). Brush both loaves with beaten egg and sprinkle with the remaining peanuts and poppy seeds. Bake in a preheated oven for 30-40 minutes until golden brown and the bread sounds hollow when tapped on the bottom.
9. Turn out the loaves and leave to cool on a wire tray.
10. Wrap in coloured cellophane paper. (Pictured on page 89.)

CHAPTER SEVEN

Here are some ideas to make your gift-wrapping sparkle – a large part of the pleasure of giving lies in the way the gift is presented.

CONTAINERS:

Make sure that any used containers which you intend to fill with edible goodies **have not been used to store toxic substances**.

Any glass, pottery or china container which is to be filled with liquids or preserves must be sterilized (see page 3).

Save all glass jars or bottles. Hunt them out at jumble sales or junk shops. Look for bottles which are an unusual shape or colour. Fill with preserves, biscuits or sweets. If the lids are missing, cover with a cellophane jam pot cover or buy cork stoppers.

Sealing wax is available from stationers in many colours. Pour melted wax over the stoppers in bottles of spiced vinegar or sloe gin.

Save boxes – shoe shops will often be pleased to give them away. Cover with paper or fabric and use to package decorated cakes.

Cake tins or pie plates are useful presents and, filled with the appropriate cake or pie, they become two presents in one.

DECORATION:

Decorate the tops of preserving jars with circles of pretty fabric cut out with pinking shears. Secure the fabric tops with an elastic band and a length of ribbon.

Save small pieces of string, ribbon, lace and sequins, beads and buttons. These can be used to decorate boxes, tins or jars which are slightly damaged.

Glue shells or dried flowers on to boxes or tins.

Decorate the top of a box with ribbon streamers: to make these, wrap ribbon tightly around the length of a pencil; spray with hairspray. Leave to dry and then carefully remove the pencil.

Paper doilys make an attractive edge to boxes or tins.

Instead of attaching a label, draw a name in glue on the outside of glass bottles or jars. Sprinkle with glitter and leave to dry.

A selection of packaging ideas, including unusual bottles, decorated jars and boxes, bows, ribbons, doilies, bought and home-made labels.

IDEAS:

Collect together several bottles, jars and tins of edible goodies. Pack into a hamper for a really special present.

A small bowl or dish looks lovely filled with tiny cakes or sweets, covered with cellophane and tied with ribbon.

Use coloured card or paper doilys to divide chocolate boxes into sections.

Arrange sweets in shallow boxes in a pattern – circles of plain and milk chocolates, for example – or pick out an initial in a contrasting colour or shape of sweet.

Make large paper cones out of pretty paper and fill with sweets. (Make as for the piping bag without snipping off the end, see page 4).

Wrap sweets or biscuits in coloured cellophane paper, twisting the paper at each end. (Coloured cellophane is available from stationers.)

At Christmas hang sweets and biscuits wrapped in cellophane paper on a small tree to make an attractive present.

Cut the pictures from old Christmas or birthday cards using pinking shears to give a crinkly edge. Punch a hole in one corner and thread through a piece of string or ribbon for instant labels.

No time to make a present? Layer different coloured pasta or nuts in a large glass jar and tie ribbon around the neck.

Remember to look at the range of packaging available at your local Marks and Spencer store for ideas.

FONDANT BOX

**Makes I Box 13 × 18 × 5 cm
(5 × 7 × 2 inches)**

*750 g (1¾ lb) fondant icing
(page 4)*

cornflour, for rolling

Preparation time: I hour,
plus I week drying
Storage time: I year,
wrapped in tissue paper
and stored in a dry room

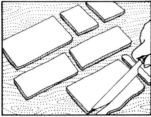

*Cutting out the six fondant icing
shapes*

*Attaching the sides to the base
of the box*

*Attaching the ends to the sides
and base*

1. Knead the icing until smooth on a
surface dusted with cornflour. Roll to a
thickness of not less than 5 mm (¼ inch).
2. Cut out the following shapes:
   2 pieces measuring 13 × 18 cm (5 × 7
   inches) (top and bottom);
   2 pieces measuring 13 × 5 cm (5 × 2
   inches) (short sides);
   2 pieces measuring 17 × 5 cm (6½ ×
   2 inches) (long sides).
Wrap the remaining fondant icing in cling
film until needed.
3. Carefully lift the shapes with a fish slice
on to sheets of non-stick silicone paper
dusted with cornflour. Lightly cover with
a cloth and leave to dry in a warm place
for 5 days. Check if the shapes are dry; if
not, leave for a few more days.
4. Place the remaining fondant, or 50 g
(2 oz), in a small bowl. Add a few drops
of warm water and beat with a wooden
spoon, adding a little more water until the
icing will spread.
5. When dry, carefully remove the
fondant shapes from the greaseproof
paper. Spread a little icing along 3 edges
of the side pieces. Press the pieces on to
the base, holding for a few minutes until
the icing begins to harden. Trim away any
excess icing with a sharp knife. Cover
with a cloth and leave to dry for 2 days in
a warm room. The basic box is now
ready for use.
6. Fill the fondant box with sweets or
chocolates. Cover with the remaining
shape as a lid and secure with ribbon. The
box can be painted with food colourings
or decorated with a design. Pipe rosettes
of royal icing along the edges or decorate
with sweets.

Right: The finished box

BUTTERFLY BOW   Use self-adhesive ribbon

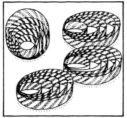

1. *Make 5 ribbon circles, decreasing in size. Place them one inside the other.*

2. *Stick the circles together at one point and press into an oval. This forms 1 wing. Repeat another 3 times.*

3. *Arrange the wings as shown in the diagram and stick on a length of ribbon, shaped at the ends, for the body and 2 thin strips for the antennae.*

MAKING A CARDBOARD BOX

If you have a shop-bought gift box which has become a little tatty, use it as a pattern to make a new one. Choose some attractive card, open the box out flat and follow the steps below to produce a smart gift box at a fraction of the cost of buying one.

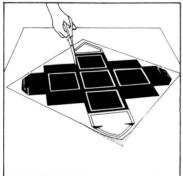

Cutting the shape out of a sheet of pretty card

Scoring lines to mark the folds

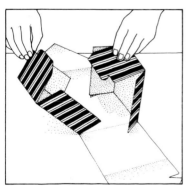

Constructing the box

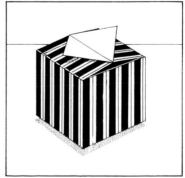

The assembled cardboard box

INDEX

Almond paste:
    colouring 3
    marbling 4
Apples, toffee 87

Birthday cracker 47
Birthday gift tags 39
Biscuits:
    Lip-shaped biscuits 26
    Oaty hearts 24
    Thank you biscuits 48
Blackberries:
    Blackberry vinegar 18
    Three-fruit jam 80
Blackcurrants:
    Three-fruit jam 80
Bon voyage gâteau 53
Bootee, christening 54
Boozy fruits 60
Bottles, preserving:
    sealing 3
    sterilizing 3
Boxes:
    cardboard 95
    decorating 91
    fondant 94
Butter:
    Orange brandy butter 13
Butterfly bow (ribbon) 95

Cake decorations 3, 64-5
Cake plaques 9
Cakes:
    Bon voyage gâteau 53
    Carrot cake 88
    Chocolate torte 76-7
    Christening bootee 54
    Desert island cake 50-2
    Glacé fruit cake 74-5
    Mini Christmas cakes 6
    Racing track cake 42
    Simnel cake 34
    Swimming pool cake 68
    Tunis cake 14
    Viennese whirls 82
Candied pumpkin 19
Cardboard box, making a 95
Cards (edible):
    Christmas card 8
    Get well soon card 70-1
    Grandma's birthday card
      40-1
    'L' plate card 49
Carrot cake 88
Cheese:
    Garlic cheese 57
    Nutty cheese breads 90
Chocolate:
    Cake decorations 65
    Chocolate torte 76-7
    Easter egg monsters 30
    Muesli chocolate cones 29
    Sweets in a shell 27
Christening bootee 54
Christmas cakes, mini 6
Christmas card, edible 8
Christmas gift tags 11
Chutney, plum 81
Coconut ice 84
Colourings, food:
    helpful tips 3
Conserve, raspberry and
    almond 60
Containers 91, 92
    decorating 91, 95
    edible 27, 94
Cracker, birthday 47

Curd, grapefruit and lime 61

Damson cheese 59
Decorations, cake 3, 64-5
Desert island cake 50-2

Easter chicks 33
Easter egg monsters 30
Easter nests 32

Father's Day relish 34
Fish, gingerbread 78
Fondant box 94
Fondant icing 4
    marbling 4
Food colouring:
    helpful tips 3
Fruit:
    Rumtopf 62
    Sparkling fruit tarts 84
    Tropical relish 16
Fudge, jigsaw 38
Fudge-topped gingerbread 83

Garlic cheese 57
Get well soon card 70-1
Gift tags, edible 11, 39
Gin:
    Raspberry gin 19
    Sloe gin 19
Gingerbread:
    Fudge-topped gingerbread
      83
    Gingerbread fish 78
    Gingerbread house 44-5
Glacé cherries:
    Liqueur cherry surprises 25
Glacé fruit cake 74-5
Grandma's birthday card 40-1
Grapefruit and lime curd 61
Grapes:
    Sparkling fruit tarts 84

Honey toffee 66

Iced bells (cake decorations)
    64-5
Icing:
    colouring 3
    Fondant icing 4
    making icing bag 4
Improvised presents 93
Indian pickle, hot 16-17

Jam, three-fruit 80
Jars, preserving:
    decorating 91
    sealing 3
    sterilizing 3
Jelly, sage 80
Jigsaw fudge 38

Labels, edible 11, 39
Labels, instant 93
Lemon creams 29
Lip-shaped biscuits 26
Liqueur cherry surprises 25
'L' plate card 49

Marmalade, tipsy 56
Mice, sugar 86
Mincemeat, whisky 20
Muesli chocolate cones 29

Nuts:
    Nut toffee 66
    Nutty cheese breads 90
    Nutty teabread 72
    Spiced nuts 88
    Swiss nut tart 73

Oaty hearts 24
Oranges:
    Orange brandy butter 13
    Orange Turkish delight 22
    Spiced oranges 20
    Tipsy marmalade 56

Peaches in brandy 21
Pickle, hot Indian 16-17
Pineapple butter 59
Plum chutney 81
Plum puddings, mini 12
Pumpkin:
    Candied pumpkin 19
Pumpkin pie 36

Racing track cake 42
Raspberry and almond
    conserve 60
Raspberry gin 19
Redcurrants:
    Three-fruit jam 80
Relish:
    Father's Day relish 34
    Tropical relish 16
Ribbon butterfly bow 95
Roses (cake decorations) 64
Royal icing 3
Rumtopf 62
Rum truffles 66

Sage jelly 80
Scottish black bun 15
Simnel cake 34
Sloe gin 19
Sparkling fruit tarts 84
Spiced nuts 88
Spiced oranges 20
Sugar mice 86
Sweets:
    containers for 92-3
    Sweets in a shell 27
Swimming pool cake 68
Swiss nut tart 73

Tarragon vinegar 58
Teabread, nutty 72
Thank you biscuits 48
Three-fruit jam 80
Tipsy marmalade 56
Toffee:
    Honey toffee 66
    Nut toffee 66
    Toffee apples 87
Tropical relish 16
Truffles, rum 66
Tunis cake 14
Turkish delight, orange 22

Viennese whirls 82
Vinegar:
    Blackberry vinegar 18
    Tarragon vinegar 58

Whisky mincemeat 20